James William Buel

The Great Operas

The Romantic Legends Upon Which the Masters of Song Have Founded...

James William Buel

The Great Operas
The Romantic Legends Upon Which the Masters of Song Have Founded...

ISBN/EAN: 9783744793018

Printed in Europe, USA, Canada, Australia, Japan

Cover: Foto ©Thomas Meinert / pixelio.de

More available books at **www.hansebooks.com**

The Great Operas

The Romantic Legends upon which
the Masters of Song have Founded
Their Famous Lyrical Compositions

INTRODUCED BY
GIUSEPPE VERDI
LAST OF THE GREAT COMPOSERS

Edited by
JAMES W BUEL, Ph.D

The Société Universelle Lyrique

London   Paris   Berlin   Philadelphia

Introduction.

By Giuseppe Verdi,
Author of
"La Traviata," "Il Trovatore,"
"Rigoletto," "Aida,"
Etc.

THE pursuit of education may not be confined to the acquisition of book-knowledge, for in its true and higher sense education is elevation of the moral and intellectual perceptions, instigating to those lofty aims that lead to all the pleasurable attainments imagination pictures. Babbling brooks and hedge choristers have voices that teach scarcely less effectively receptive and contemplative minds than does the most learned preceptor, for song is the universal language of aspiration, which begets the master artisan who builds the splendid castles of our dreams. The first invocation was the ejaculation, "Oh God!" The human ear, however, was quick to catch the sweet harmonies that welled from warblers of the woods, and by these our primitive progenitors were taught to chant their orisons:

> "With heavenly touch of instrumental sound
> In full harmonic number joined, their songs
> Divide the night, and lift our thoughts to heaven."

Music and poetry are arts that appeal to heart and soul, stirring the savage to manifestations of ecstacy, as well as moving with feelings of delight the most cultured and refined. In this respect music is the art of arts, the alphabet and the science, the incentive and the crown of that education which is the surest promotive of good citizenship, as well as of enjoyment.

The story-writer has been the greatest contributor to the world's entertainment, but the song-writer has added most to the world's pleasure; the two conjoining their

INTRODUCTION.

talents have had immeasurable influence in elevating and refining all peoples, and hence all nations. National hymns have powerfully re-enforced national armies, for they may be said to be not merely stimulative, but creators of patriotism. Religion is not less benefited by psalmody, and the domestic hearth is made dearer to us by songs in the family circle.

The supreme type of music is the opera, because it represents the marriage of story and song, a union of those twin arts which approach so nearly the divine, a veritable apostrophe of that poetic sentiment which we feel in the stillness of isolation, and which burns with fiercer glow under the thrilling serenade of the grand concert. Opera is quite as dependent upon story as upon music, and while the ear is always pleased with sweet sounds, a proper appreciation of opera is not possible without a knowledge of the tale which it unfolds by song. It has, therefore, long been a matter of much surprise that the music-loving people of all countries have given so little study to the tales of the operas which have pleased them. True, it is, librettos are always on sale, but as a rule they are so little regarded that it is hardly exaggerating the facts to say scarcely one person in ten is familiar with the stories of the most famous operas. With much gratification do I therefore hail the publication of THE GREAT OPERAS as a work that supplies an imperative need to cultured persons. I believe this excellent book will be of real value to the whole musical world. The tales herein will be of infinite value by way of cultivating an interest in opera among the masses, for readers thereof will be afforded such pleasure that desire will be created to hear the operatic dramatizations, and thus the holy influence of song and story will be graciously diffused, to the pleasure and benefit of all peoples.

[*Translation from the Italian.*]

G. Verdi

To the Memory of

Giuseppe Verdi

This Edition of The Great Operas is

Dedicated

as a fitting tribute of the loving regard and lofty appreciation

of the whole civilized world,

not only for

his Masterly Contributions to Musical Art,

but also for his

Philanthropic spirit manifested by the Founding and Munificent

Endowment of two Splendid Homes, in

Milan and Villa Sinova, Italy

for aged and indigent musicians.

The Publishers

Contents of Section One

THE INTRODUCTION.	BY GIUSEPPE VERDI
A LIFE-SKETCH OF GIUSEPPE VERDI	
LA TRAVIATA,	BY GIUSEPPE VERDI
A SKETCH OF RICHARD WAGNER	
TANNHAUSER.	BY RICHARD WAGNER
A SKETCH OF AMBROISE THOMAS	
MIGNON.	BY AMBROISE THOMAS
A SKETCH OF CHARLES FRANCOIS GOUNOD	
FAUST,	BY CHARLES FRANCOIS GOUNOD
A SKETCH OF PIETRO MASCAGNI	
CAVALLERIA RUSTICANA.	BY PIETRO MASCAGNI
THE RHINEGOLD.	BY RICHARD WAGNER
THE VALKYRIE.	BY RICHARD WAGNER
SIEGFRIED.	BY RICHARD WAGNER
GOTTERDAMMERUNG.	BY RICHARD WAGNER
SKETCH OF FRIEDRICH VON FLOTOW	
STRADELLA.	BY FRIEDRICH VON FLOTOW

A BRIEF HISTORY OF OPERA.

IT IS not a difficult thing to write a history of Opera, because it requires no long search through ancient records, composed in dead languages, to find its origin and beginning, for it had no existence five centuries ago. It is a poor antiquarian, however, who cannot present some archaic example of every modern thought, or a rusty key to every discovery or accomplishment of the age, by reference to venerable annals of the remote past; and thus we are told by some musical pundits that the origin of Opera may be found in the Greek Plays. Without pausing to dispute, I will venture the opinion that there is no more connection between the Greek Plays and Opera, than there is between the gem through which Nero viewed the tragedies of the Coliseum, and the telescope. At least one of the Jesuit fathers, Menestrier, declares that the Song of Solomon was operatic, and cites a passage in St. Jerome's "Origen" in support of this declaration. But these opinions, while interesting, are really of small value, for they are not in accord with the present understanding of what constitutes Opera. It is true, however, that this form of music was first employed by the Church, as was Oratorio, the earliest rendering of which was "The Conversion of St. Paul," played in music at Rome in 1440. It is important to note that both the spoken and the lyric drama had their origin and earliest representations in Italy, for the fact is well authenticated that the first profane subject rendered operatically was "Orpheus," the composition of which was by Angelo Poliziano, and the libretto by Cardinal Riario, who was nephew of Sixtus IV. This opera was produced in Rome in 1480, in a theatre maintained by the Popes. Thus it is proper to observe that the sacred musical plays of the Fifteenth Century gradually developed, under patronage of the Church, into Grand Opera, which presently took a wide scope that comprehended quite as much of the profane as the sacred.

The happy conception of the lyric drama was quickly followed by substantial benefits to the Church, for it served to increase popular interest, and the influence of this new form of dramatic music was extended by scenic accessories, which were presently employed with striking effects in the musical representations. We are told that this new art developed so rapidly that early in the Sixteenth Century Peruzzi, a decorator of the Papal theatre, astonished the greatest painters of his time by his marvelous scenic illusions, which appeared so real in their solidity and perspective that Titian himself was not satisfied that the painted representations of houses, porticos, and profiles were deceptive, until he had mounted a ladder and touched the canvas with his own hands. The operas which were thus splendidly produced—at least so far as scenic effects could make them splendid—in the first century of their introduction, were no doubt of an impressive character, but it is not an easy matter now to discover the subjects thus lyrically treated, for the history of music is not so complete as to have preserved the story of these early productions; it is probable, too, that the works thus performed were, to an extent, experimental and semi-private, so that we must admit a hiatus in the record of nearly a century, or until 1597, in which year the opera of "Daphne" was performed in the Corsi Palace, at Florence, the music of which was composed by Peri and Caccini, and the libretto by the distinguished poet Rinuccini. It appears that this was the first complete opera, but it was a masterpiece of both dramatic and music writing which met with such pronounced success

LISZT PLAYING BEFORE WAGNER AND OTHER GERMAN COMPOSERS.

that the same authors, three years later, composed the opera of "Eurydice," in five acts, which was likewise performed in the Corsi Palace, in honor of the marriage of Maria de Medici to Henry IV. of France. The popularity of this new creation was so great that imitators sprang up, and a wave of operatic enthusiasm fairly overflowed northern Italy, under

A BRIEF HISTORY OF OPERA

which stimulus not a few worthy composers contested for public favor. And, yet, while "Daphne" was operatic, it bore small relation to the song drama of to-day, for the dialogue was all recitative, and it was only at the conclusion of each act that the chorus was heard.

Following the history of opera, which properly had its beginning in the production of "Daphne," Gagliano wrote a new score to Rinuccini's libretto, which had a successful performance at Mantua in 1608, and twenty years later the piece was translated by Opitz, who is called "father of the lyric stage in Germany," with music by Schutz, and performed at Dresden on the occasion of the marriage of the Landgrave of Hesse with the sister of John—George I, Elector of Saxony.

Monteverde's first operatic production was "Arianna," a very meritorious work, which was printed in 1607, followed by his "Orpheus" in 1608, both of which were performed in Venice with the accessories of an orchestra of thirty-nine mixed instruments including brass, wood and string, and the effect was a new sensation that at once established the composer in the affections of all lovers of music, and brought him also the substantial honors that fall to the acknowledged head of a new school, for he had imitators and pupils by the score. One of these latter was the subsequently famous Cavalli, who introduced the aria as a relief to the monotonous recitative, but the suggestion of this feature is found in an air which Monteverde used in his "Orpheus," which the devoted husband sings while leading his "Eurydice" back to life from the abode of death. It is interesting to observe that Monteverde employed instruments, some of which are now obsolete, the tones of which accorded strikingly with the character of the dialogue and emphasized the sentiment of the subject. Thus in his "Orpheus," the base viola accompanied the recitative of his hero; the violas played to the voice of "Eurydice;" the trombones followed Pluto; and the organ assisted Apollo; but, to our surprise, the guitar was considered by this great composer to be a fitting instrumental accessory to the declamations of Charon. Other instruments, which he adapted to the chorus, were double harps, violins, flutes, clarions, and trombones. His work was so masterful, so soulfully impressive, that not only did the Church of St. Mark, of which he was chapel-master, promote his operas by magnificent performances, but through his influence theatres were built in Venice, Rome, Bologna, Turin, Naples and Messina, which were munificently patronized by popes, cardinals, dukes, and the most illustrious nobles of the century.

To Cavalli must the credit be given for introducing musical imitations of the sounds of nature, which was a decided and pleasing advance; while about the same time Cesti, another Venetian composer, invented the da capo—repetition of the first part of the aria—which proved to be a delightful resource that was destined to be retained for all time.

A form of entertainment so pleasing, influential and popular as opera had now become, could not be long confined exclusively to the nation of its birth, and directly after its establishment in so many of the large cities of Italy, demand was made for its introduction into France. Cardinal Mazarin was ordered by Richelieu to visit the principal cities of Italy, and to make a study of the operas there performed, with the view of acquiring knowledge that would be serviceable in presenting some of the tragedies written by the Cardinal-Minister in France. The result of these visits made by Abbe Mazarin was the establishment (1645) of French Opera under Cambert, and his distinguished successor, Lulli; but, strange to relate, for a hundred years there was maintained a fierce rivalry in France between the partisans of the French and Italian schools, which culminated in 1752 by a hostile demonstration in Paris against Pergolese's "La Serva Padrona," that drove the two chief singers in the piece from Paris. This prejudice, which broke in such violence, did not end with this outcry against Italian Opera, however, for it served to create an enmity against Cambert, who had received a charter from Louis XIV. (1669), giving him a monopoly of opera houses in France, that caused a revocation of his privilege and its transference to Giovanni Lulli, whereupon Cambert retired to England, where he became master of the King's band (Charles II.). Lulli was both competent and industrious, and a genius as well, but while he wrote no less than twenty operas in fourteen years, all of which were produced in Paris on a scale of almost astonishing magnificence, he was not a master of melody, nor was he a great creator of effects, unless we except the kind of overture which he introduced—to be afterwards perfected by

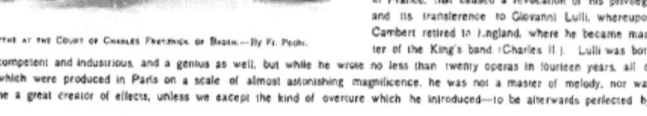

Goethe at the Court of Charles Frederick of Baden.—By Fr. Pecht.

Handel, but he was a genius in respect of his humor and acute appreciation of the tricks that please the public, and he was not lacking in the merits of a painstaking and effective composer and leader. His death occurred at the age of fifty-four (1687), caused by an injury to his foot, the result of a blow of his walking-stick, given in a moment of intense enthusiasm during a performance of a Te Deum he had composed to celebrate the convalescence of Louis XIV.

The influence of Lulli was so great that it extended from the throne to the gutter, under which the great Louis was induced to become both an actor and a singer on the stage of Grand Opera, one of his favorite characters being The Sun, in "Flora," in which he appeared no less than eighteen times, while many persons of the nobility assumed similar parts without "derogating from their titles or immunities." The craze became finally so great that both men and women might, by royal process, or *lettres de cachet*, be compelled to take parts in the operas, which conscriptions were made like those for the army and navy.

Italian composers led the way to the introduction of opera in Germany, as they did in France, and in the first decade of the Seventeenth Century they were received with much cordiality by the Court of Saxony. Progress was, however, prevented in this direction by the Thirty Years' War, so that opera was not finally established

Beethoven's Dream. By A. de Lemus.

in Germany until the production of Purcell's "Dido and Æneas," in Hamburg, in 1678. It is true that three pieces of little consequence were produced a year earlier in that city, but they had no success and are now entirely forgotten. "Dido," on the contrary, was received with great favor, and to its popular presentation is due the permanent establishment of the opera in Hamburg. The interest was local despite its intensity, and it was not until many years after that other German cities came to the support of this form of entertainment. Frederick the Great, who was musician, as well as warrior, is responsible for the introduction of Italian Opera in Berlin; his favorite composers were Hasse, Agricola, and Graun, and so devoted was he to the art that he supported the opera from his own private purse, and even officiated as general conductor of an orchestra of fifty pieces. German Opera may be said to have been perfected by Keiser, whose first production, in 1692, when he was only nineteen years of age, gave strength to the movement which had made little progress before. His first composition, entitled "Ismene," was of a pastoral nature, and met with a moderate success; but his second, called "Basilius," was pure opera of unquestioned merit that brought him into favorable notice as one having talent of a glorious promise. These two pieces had their presentations at the Court of Wolfenbuttel and were not repeated elsewhere, but their influence was sufficiently great to draw public attention to the possibilities of opera in Germany, and to arouse an interest that led to its establishment in that country at the large theatres, and which, in its higher development, gave to the world not a few of the most illustrious composers of which music and civilization alike can boast.

The founding of opera in England is credited to the patronage of both the Lord Protector and Charles II., but this contention no doubt grows out of the intense hatreds that existed between the Royalists, or Cavaliers, and the Round Heads, or Ironsides, neither party being willing to concede any honor whatever to the other. Cromwell was so devoted to music that he kept in his own service some of the most skillful performers of his time, and it was by his special permission that opera was established in England; but the representations given under his patronage were few and of small consequence. Charles II., however, was such an enthusiastic lover of music that he took pains to promote the art in many ways, and upon the coming to London of Cambert, the King received him with evidence of the highest favor. Cambert was the father of French Opera, who transplanted his system to England, where it flourished under the fostering care of the Court until it became a popular institution. The music of Cambert's "Pomona," and of his "Pains and Pleasures of Love," thoroughly established the composer in the affections of the English, a popularity which he retained until his death, in 1677. Cambert has been given the credit of establishing French Opera in England, but the honor does not wholly belong to him of being the founder of that form of entertainment in that country, for as early as 1656

Sir William Davenant obtained a permit under which he opened a theatre for operatic performances in Aldersgate street Long before this, too, there were entertainments of an operatic character at the Court masques of James I. and Charles I., under the directorship of Laniere, who was both musician and painter of much fame.

The first English opera produced at Davenant's Theatre was the "Siege of Rhodes," at which the story was sung in recitative, and it was not until fifteen years later (1671) that the first performance of Cambert's "Pomona" took place. But English Opera took its impetus from the master work of Purcell, who composed the music to Dryden's librettos of "Dido and Æneas" (1677), "The Tempest" (1690), "King Arthur" (1691), "The Prophetess" (1693), and several others, and of whom Dr Burney thus writes: "There is a latent power and force in his (Purcell's) expression of English words, whatever be the subject, that will make an unprejudiced native of this island feel more than all the elegance, grace and refinement of modern music, less happily applied, can do; and this pleasure is communicated to us, not by the symmetry or rhythm of modern melody, but by his having tuned to the true accents of our mother tongue those notes of passion which an inhabitant of this island would breathe in such situations as the words describe. Handel, who flourished in a less barbarous age of art, has been acknowledged Purcell's superior in many particulars; but in none more than the art and grandeur of his choruses, the harmony and texture of his organ fugues, as well as his great style of concertos; the ingenuity of his accompaniments to his songs and choruses; and even in the general melody of the airs themselves; yet, in the accent, passion and expression of English words, the vocal music of Purcell is, sometimes, to my feelings, as superior to Handel as an original poem to a translation."

Italian Opera was introduced into England very early in the Eighteenth Century, but it made small progress until the coming of Handel to London in 1710, under whom it advanced so rapidly as to speedily gain a firm hold upon popular favor, which has never since been relinquished, notwithstanding the long and severe criticisms which Addison fulminated against its incongruities in the "Spectator."

In the United States there is no school of Grand Opera, because Republican forms of government take no concern in the maintenance of amusements, but nevertheless Americans are provided with abundant opportunities for enjoying the productions of the masters who have written in the Italian, German and English, and they are accordingly well informed,

MASTERS OF GERMAN MUSIC.— By W. Lindenschmidt.

though not to the point, perhaps, of critical judgment, as to the merits of the several European schools. Patronage has been generous, especially to Italian Grand Opera, in America, and the German composers of first rank are as familiar to cultured persons in the great Republic as they are to the nobility of the Old World.

It is remarkable how such a foreign accessory as the *ballet divertissement* could be so firmly connected with Grand Opera, though in Opera Bouffe it might be made a natural feature. Yet the fact remains, inconsistent though it appears, that the ballet has been regarded as an inseparable accompaniment, particularly in French Opera, almost since the introduction of the lyrical drama into France. In the middle of the Sixteenth Century ballets were performed at the French Court, having been introduced by an Italian named Baltasarini, in a celebration of the marriage of the Duke de Joyeuse, and so magnificent was the presentation that the cost is said to have exceeded $700,000. In the early representations, however, there were no females in the ballet, those parts being taken by young boys and dancing masters, all of whom wore masks. The first *corps de ballet* in which women appeared was organized in 1681, to present "The Triumph of Love," in which Madame la Dauphine, Princess de Conti and Mdlle. de Nantes, supported by the Dauphin, the Prince de Conti and the Duke de Vermandois, were the principal dancers, since which time, and especially after Lulli became manager of the Academy, the ballet has

A BRIEF HISTORY OF OPERA

been an inseparable feature of all French Operas. The Duchess du Maine had the honor of inventing the dramatic ballet, which became so popular in France that it was presently carried to England; its success in that country, however, has never been pronounced, though it still frequently appears there, but as an exotic which may never become acclimated.

Opera Bouffe is a natural outgrowth of Grand Opera, though its origin is not definitely traceable, nor its creator positively known. The first mention made of the performance of a musical comedy that I have been able to find, is by Milton, who states that he attended the presentation of "Chi Soffre Speri," which was given at Florence in 1639, under the patronage of Cardinal Barberini, and in 1657 a theatre was opened in Florence devoted exclusively to Opera Bouffe, but it proved such a failure that no effort was made to revive the entertainment until the following century, when what is known as the Neapolitan school accomplished its successful revivification. "La Serva Padrona" was perhaps the first thoroughly popular comic opera that was produced, its introduction having been made in Rome, in 1735, with such triumph that it was taken to Paris in 1750, and thence to other countries, and everywhere received with applause. The new art became even more popular in France than in Italy, and was soon permanently established there in the Theatre de l'Opera Comique, or Salle Favart, which was devoted to this light form of entertainment, and thence it spread to other countries to endure as a permanent feast for art and music lovers.

MOZART AND HIS SISTER PLAYING BEFORE MARIE THERESE — By A. Borckmar.

Stage decoration is a matter of probably greater consequence than either score or libretto, for objects which appeal to the eye are more impressive than is the influence of sounds, however harmonious, to the ear; but while opera, as a purely musical art, has made wonderful progress, in scenic effects there has been no advance, perhaps because education of the ear has been such as to leave less need for magnificent aids to the understanding. Whatever may be the reasons, certain it is, that stage decoration, in the mounting of the greatest operas, is not carried to the extent now that it was one or even two centuries ago. Servandoni, at the Theatre of the Tuileries, which had a seating capacity of seven thousand persons, introduced such mechanical devices as are no longer employed, because of their elaborateness and expense. In Vienna, where Italian Opera was established under Emperor Leopold I., stage decoration was carried to a point where the word magnificence scarcely describes it. Lady Montague, writing to the Pope of a performance she attended in Vienna, in 1716, says:

"I have been last Sunday at the opera, which was performed in the Garden of the Favorita; and I was so much pleased with it. I have not yet repented of my seeing it. Nothing of the kind was ever more magnificent, and I can easily believe what I am told, that the decorations and habits cost the Emperor thirty thousand pounds sterling. The stage was built over a large canal, and at the beginning of the second act divided into two parts, discovering the water, on which there immediately came, from different parts, two fleets of little gilded vessels, that gave the representation of a naval fight. It is not easy to imagine the beauty of this scene, which I took particular notice of. * * * The story of the opera is the enchantment of 'Alcina,' which gives opportunities for a great variety of machines, and changes of scenes which are performed with surprising swiftness. The theatre is so large that it is hard to carry the eye to the end of it, and the habits in the utmost magnificence to the number of one hundred and eight."

In the early years of the Seventeenth Century many large open-air theatres were built for the presentation of spectacular opera, one of which, at Parma, now a ruin, had a capacity for fifty thousand spectators. Servandoni painted many admirable scenes for the Opera House in Dresden, which had a stage so large that four hundred mounted horsemen were able to manœuvre with ease upon it. Bernino, an Italian architect, sculptor and painter, has the credit of having produced sunsets that completely deceived whole audiences, and in a spectacular piece of his composition, entitled "The Inundation of the Tiber," realism was perfected by his representation of a great mass of water rushing from the back of the stage with such force as to appear to be sweeping everything before it, until the startled spectators, believing the inundation to be real, rushed in terror from the theatre. Nor was the scene only a painter's simulation, for a vast volume of water was really let loose, but just before reaching the orchestra it was turned into traps sufficiently large to allow the whole to escape without doing any damage.

In operas produced at Venice, animated scenes were presented that exhibited grand hunts, charges of cavalry, triumphal processions composed of hundreds of horsemen; and even ships were shown moving under full sail across the ocean, all with such perfect imitation that it was often with difficulty the large audiences could bring themselves to believe they were viewing only theatrical illusions.

These magnificent spectacles were necessary in their day, when opera was undergoing its metamorphosis, but while the eye still seeks gratification, the other senses have been educated until opera is not only intelligible, but affords a pleasure graduated to the comprehension of the eye and intelligence. We now look less towards the scenery than we listen to the strains of the orchestra and the voice of the singer, in which our greatest delight is found, a gratification which remains long after the curtain is rung down.

Opera has been introduced so recently into the New World that it can scarcely be said to have a history that deserves more than a passing reference to its representation under the direction of contemporary impresarios. But although as yet very young, the growth of opera sentiment in America is both rapid and substantial, with promise of great attainment, even without the encouragement of national subventions, such as is given by nearly all the countries of Europe. To such indefatigable, intelligent and masterly directors as Grau, Damrosch, Mapleson, Thomas, opera in America is indebted for its establishment as an institution, which is fast gaining the affection of the masses, and which may now be regarded as a permanency. And the benefits are pronounced, for there is clearly discernible a growing interest in musical art, such as only the lyric drama fosters, manifested by an increase of audiences, the building of larger and finer opera houses, and a distinct advance in educated sentiment that foreshadows a gratifying culmination. Festivals of song have become almost as frequent among Americans as in European centres of culture, and patronage of the best representations of Grand Opera has grown to such proportions that the New World is denied nothing which the Old World has to offer.

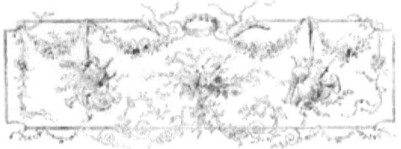

BEETHOVEN AT THE HOUSE OF MOZART   By C. Herpfer

It has not escaped comment that America has produced no composer of Grand Opera who is entitled to rank among the great, but this fact should not prejudice opinion against the probability that one may soon appear, for the subject claims so much attention among the musically cultured that essays are numerous, and promising results have already been attained. But while Americans are waiting the appearance of a famous composer, they point with pride to many prima donnas, born of the Western World, whose voices charm the listening ears of Europe, and whose virtues no less than their gifts, honor the country of their birth.

A LIFE SKETCH OF VERDI.

IT IS neither claiming too much, nor offering a panegyric of extravagant praise, to represent Verdi as incomparably the greatest living composer in the opera world. Neither would it transcend the limits of justice to declare that his position is at the front, among the very few who rank as the most renowned musical geniuses that any age has produced. His life has been long spared, nor have four-score years brought upon him the mental decline which is so often shadowed forth in vain attempts made by venerable intellects to increase successes won in the mid-day of physical prime. Fortune has been specially kind to this distinguished master, for his mental gifts raised him out of all the disadvantages of lowly birth and bore him upward, without halt, to a goal which many strive to attain but which only one in a century manages to reach. Genius, however, has not been his only endowment, for this is often erratic and joined to a nature that betrays ignoble traits; to him the honor is doubly great, for noble manhood is no less conspicuous in his character than is masterful proficiency marked in his works, which prove him to be both good and great.

Giuseppe Verdi was born October 9, 1814, in the village of Roncole, near Busseto, in the duchy of Parma, Italy. His father was a modest innkeeper who, though not unappreciative of the benefits of education, was unable, for lack of means, to give his children the advantages which private instructors afford, and he was therefore compelled by circumstances to trust them to the care of the village schools. Giuseppe very early manifested a passion for music, to gratify which he was allowed to become the pupil of an organist who played in the town church on Sundays and gave lessons to a small class during week-days. The young man made such excellent use of his limited opportunities for musical culture, that he attracted the attention of a rich gentleman of Parma, named Antonio Barezzi, who, in 1833, offered to pay the expense of his instruction at the Conservatory in Milan. This generous proposal was eagerly seized by Giuseppe, but his happy hopes were disappointed by failure to pass the necessary examination for admission. His kind benefactor again came to the aid of the ambitious pupil in the hour of his deep distress, by placing him under the instruction of an excellent musician named Lavigna, who at the time was a member of the orchestra of the La Scala Theatre in Milan. Under this teacher's direction young Verdi continued for several years, giving his principal attention to operatic composition, in which he showed such advancement that in 1839 he was encouraged to permit the public production of his first piece, entitled "Oberto di San Bonifazio." The success of this maiden effort was not great, yet sufficient to stimulate him to other trials, and two years later he composed "Un Giorno di Regno," which to his mortification was a sad failure. A less ambitious man might have been crushed by such a result, but Verdi's character now showed itself in its full strength, for failure in one effort determined him to try with persistent purpose until victory should be won. Nor was his reward long delayed, for in 1842 he produced his third composition, "Nabucco," which was characterized by such brilliancy, melody and dramatic effect that the audience was fairly transported with ecstasy, and his fame was established at one bound. The name of Verdi was heard on everybody's lips in Milan, "Nabucco" was repeated time and time again, and in less than one month after the initial performance the opera became the rage all over Italy, and soon afterwards was heard in many of the capitals of Europe.

Giuseppe Verdi.

A LIFE SKETCH OF VERDI

In 1843 Verdi produced "I Lombardi," which scored an immediate success, not a few musicians pronouncing it superior to his "Nabucco." His versatility, industry, and genius were thereafter exhibited in the rapidity with which he wrote, no less than four grand operas being produced by him in 1844-45, and each a pronounced success. These, in the order of their composition, were "Ernani," "I due Foscari," "Giovanna d'Arco," and "Alzira," all of which were brought out in Venice and received with universal praise, though "Ernani" is the only one of the four that has survived its early popularity. In 1846 Verdi's ninth opera, "Attila," was given in Venice, but coldly received; his next production, however, "Macbeth," which was produced at Florence, in 1847, was attended by extraordinary demonstrations of praise. The author was called before the curtain no less than thirty times at three successive performances, and not content with these marks of favor, the populace insisted on forming triumphal processions to escort him to and from the theatre, the several forms of popular laudation finally culminating in a testimonial of a golden crown bestowed upon him by the city.

HOUSE IN WHICH VERDI WAS BORN

Verdi's fame was now carried beyond the confines of his own country, for in the latter part of 1847 he was induced to visit London, where, with great success, he produced his eleventh opera, "I Masnadieri," in which Jenny Lind assumed the leading role. A month later his "Lombards," under the title of "Jerusalem," was translated into French and presented at the Grand Opera in Paris, where it was most flatteringly received. He continued to compose, with indefatigable industry, and the whole of Europe rang with his praises; for though they appeared rapidly, all of his compositions exhibited evidences of almost incomparable genius. His successive works were as follows: "Il Corsaro," produced in 1848 at Trieste; "La Battaglia di Legnano," at Rome in the same year, but which was interdicted because of the political character of the story; "Luisa Miller," written in 1849, for Naples; "Stiffelio," given at Trieste in 1850; "Rigoletto," performed in Venice, 1851; "Il Trovatore," presented in Rome, 1853; "La Traviata," produced in Venice the same year; "Les Vepres Siciliennes," represented at the Grand Opera, Paris, in 1855; "Un Ballo in Maschera," given in Rome, 1859; "La forza del Destino," "Aroldo," "Simon Boccanegra," and "Una Vendetta in Domino," all performed in St. Petersburg, 1863; "Don Carlos," 1867, and "Aida," 1871, both given in Cairo, Egypt. In 1874 he composed a requiem mass for the anniversary of the death of Manzoni, which was performed under his direction in Paris, and one year later in London, his life-work being crowned by his "Otello," in 1890, and his "Falstaff," in 1893, compositions which exhibit all the strength, the charming melody and dramatic fire of his earlier years.

Verdi does not count all his honors as the recognition of his musical proficiency alone —as acknowledgments and rewards that give him the chief place among the greatest composers born in Italy—for testimonials have been showered upon him by grateful peoples who appreciate the grandeur of his noble nature as well as his masterful genius as a creator of melody. Verdi's domestic life has been eventful, with unusual diversity of joy and sorrow. In 1836 he married Margherita Barezzi, whose father, though a shopkeeper, was the man to whom Verdi is indebted most largely for his success, as before explained. Four years later, and at a time when financial difficulties most seriously opposed his ambitions, his wife, and two children, that had been born to him meantime, fell ill of fatal maladies, and within a space of two months he was bereft of all his loved ones. This great loss piled upon his lesser misfortunes, with which he had been contending almost despairingly, crushed him to the earth, from which possibly he may not have risen again but for the fact that he had solemnly contracted to compose a comic opera, which his sense of obligation would not permit him to violate. He therefore aroused himself from his deep despondency and produced "Un Giorno di Regno," which, alas, was a failure. Evil fortune, like sorrow, may be outrun by persistence, and so Verdi found it, thanks to the encouragement of his friends. Prosperity and fame at last came to him, and in these the old sorrows of bereavement and disappointment were gradually forgotten. Verdi remained a widower for more than twenty years, but his heart at last capitulated again, and he became husband to Signorina Giuseppina Strepponi, daughter of a choirmaster of Monza Cathedral, near Milan. This lady was one of the greatest sopranos of her time, and a lyrical tragedienne to whose wonderful representations, in leading roles, much of the success of Verdi's early operas is due. At the time of his second marriage, and for some years afterwards, Verdi made his home in Milan, but he subsequently removed to Genoa,

Verdi, Ricordi, his Publisher and Chiusa, the Artist

A LIFE SKETCH OF VERDI.

taking up his residence in the Palazzo Doria which he still makes his winter home. In December, 1897, his devoted wife and genial companion died of a lingering illness, leaving him alone once more, when old age had enfeebled his powers of resignation, and for more than two months his life was despaired of. Old friends, especially his publisher, Ricordi, and Boito, librettist of several of his operas, gave him such devoted attentions as caused a rally from his depression and happily he is still spared to the world, by whom he is revered as the greatest of the living masters of song. During the winter Verdi continues to reside in the Doria palace, at Genoa, where he is inaccessible except to his most intimate friends, reserving the privilege of old age to select his company; but the summer he passes at his magnificent country seat near Busseto, which is some seventy miles distant from Milan. It is the old homestead, so to speak, near the place of his birth, which he has beautified by large expenditures and thus made it delightful as well as sacred. Close by his palatial residence he has built a large and substantial theatre, in which operas are often rehearsed, and entertainments given for the pleasure of the towns-people.

Social, political and professional honors have been bestowed upon Verdi in generous bounty, not only by his own countrymen, but by rulers of many nations, though in every case these flattering marks of distinction were conferred without his seeking. In 1859 he was elected a member of the National Assembly, and in 1861 the King appointed him Senator; in 1871 he was made Minister of Public Instruction, and the following year a senatorship was again conferred upon him, but he refused to act, and resigned in order to pursue the calling for which nature so manifestly fitted him; nor has inducement since been great enough to withdraw him from this seclusion with the spirit of music. Among the other great honors bestowed upon him was his election as a member of the Legion of Honor of France, member of the Académie des Beaux Arts, member of the Academy of Fine Arts, of Prussia, appointment as Grand Officer of the Order of the Crown of Italy; and exalted decorations have been given him by the rulers of Russia, Germany, France, Turkey, Austria and Egypt.

Great as has been the career of Giuseppe Verdi, his honorable and successful life received its imperishable recognition at his own hands, for true greatness is that appreciation of self which is exhibited in providing for the comforts and pleasures of others. Such a splendid monument Verdi has prepared by setting aside the sum of 3,000,000 lire ($600,000) for a hospital at Milan, the money being placed on deposit for the purpose with the Popular Bank of that city. He has also provided for the erection and maintenance of another hospital—both intended more particularly for aged and indigent musicians—at Villa Nuova, near San Agatha, which he has endowed with the sum of 500,000 lire ($100,000).

I had the honor of being presented to the famous maestro at his home, the Palazzo Doria, in Genoa, the last day of April, 1896, a meeting having been arranged between us by several of the most distinguished composers of Europe, who had manifested an interest in the proposed publication of this work. I also carried with me letters of introduction from many persons of prominence as writers, and of high official positions, to whom I make this acknowledgment of my thanks, among whom I beg to specially mention Baron Fava, the Italian Minister to the United States; Wayne MacVeagh, United States Ambassador to Italy; Massenet, the most famous of living French composers; Marchetti, Director of St. Cecilia Conservatory, Rome; Boito, of Milan, librettist and composer; Mr. Blumenberg, editor of the *Musical Courier*; Fannie Edgar Thomas, of Paris, a famous contributor; Mr. Fletcher, United States Consul-General at Genoa, and Mr. Dobrilovitch, the secretary. I was accompanied on my visit to Verdi by Mr. Edward de Lima, of New York, a prominent business gentleman of that city, whose familiarity with all the European languages gave me invaluable assistance, for, to my mortification, I was unable to converse with the maestro in his native tongue.

VERDI AND ARRIGO BOITO

A LIFE SKETCH OF VERDI

I reached the Doria palace at noon on the day Verdi had appointed to meet me, and was cordially received. I had expected to find him bent under the burden of his eighty-two years and afflicted with such infirmities as usually show themselves in persons of great age, but to my surprise he stood before me the very embodiment of physical and intellectual vigor. He was comfortably dressed in a working jacket, and looked as though he might have just left off some pleasant labor in order to consider a business proposal. His hair was both thick and long, combed back as his pictures represent, and hung almost upon his shoulders, nor was it more than barely touched with the frosts of years. His eyes were wondrously bright and genial, and his voice was as sweet and low as a woman's; but his bearing was that of a king, not haughty, n r formal, but statuesque, grand, magnificent. I committed the impropriety of extending my hand, but he understood that the act was a solecism peculiar to Americans, and returning the greeting with much cordiality he conducted me to a seat beside a centre-table, whereupon Mr. de Lima explained the object of our call more fully than the letters which I had sent him could do. I was much gratified to find the great composer thoroughly interested in the work I had in contemplation, and during the hour or more I spent with him he gave me many valuable suggestions, which I have adopted to the great benefit of the book. He cheerfully complied with my request to write an introduction for THE GREAT OPERAS, and promised to have it ready on the following day. I was agreeably surprised to find him so enthusiastic, and little expected that he would so promptly perform so great a service, as there was no consideration involved beyond what he expressed was a pleasure to promote so beneficent an enterprise as I had undertaken, and which he declared the world had already waited for and needed too long.

FACSIMILE OF THE ORIGINAL SCORE OF THE MISERERE, in "IL TROVATORE."

I returned to Verdi's home on the day following our first interview, and to my intense satisfaction found the introductory matter ready as per his promise, for which I tendered all possible thanks, but he refused to receive them, declaring that it was he who had to thank me for the opportunity and honor I had given him to assist in the splendid work which I had in hand. After delivering to me the type-written introduction he requested its return for a moment, saying, "I feel that I have not said enough in commendation of your most praiseworthy enterprise, and must add another sentence," whereupon he wrote with pen two lines, which translated read, "I believe your work will be of especial value to the musical world." My admiration for the man is equal to that of my appreciation of his genius; for the impression which he produces is that of a knight of chivalrous mien and generous character, an ideal poet, and a creator of song, for in his face is expressed the majesty of sweetness and a noble tenderness that is ineffable.

On January 20th, 1901, Verdi, last of the great composers, whose work being ended yet lived so beloved in the hearts of all people, was seized of a cold while he was at Milan, looking after the house which he was building and had almost completed for indigent musicians. He gradually grew worse until pneumonia developed. Almost hourly bulletins were published reporting his condition, which, considering his great age, led his admirers in Europe and America to fear a fatal issue. Nor was this dread removed, for on Sunday morning of January 27th the great composer peacefully passed to his final rest, leaving the civilized world in profoundest grief, for his like we may not soon look upon again.

La Traviata

(AFTER THE ORIGINAL PAINTING BY WILLIAM DE LEFTWICH DODGE)

ALFRED—"*I call on you to witness,
Friends, that I have paid her now.*"

ACT II.—SCENE IV

LA TRAVIATA.

(THE LOST ONE.)

Music by Verdi.——Words by Piave.

A TRAVIATA is founded upon one of Dumas, Jr.'s, most popular novels, entitled "*Dame aux Camélias*" (Lady with the Camellias), best known to the English stage as "Camille," for it is presented so often in the form of a drama as an opera. But the story as adapted by Piave departs materially from Dumas' original, both in plot and incident. The Italian librettist has also taken the license to make the action of the story apply especially to the time of Louis XIV. Instead of continuing the purpose of the novelist to illustrate phases of modern French life; the operatic representation is therefore largely original, nor has the change destroyed either the influence or the dramatic effect of the story.

The action of the piece takes place in Paris and its suburbs, and the plot, which deals with the most serious affairs without suggestion of a comedy relief, is as follows: Violetta Valery is a notorious, or rather, I should say, a famous member of the Paris demi-monde, whose attractiveness lies as much in her intellectual accomplishments and vivacity of manner as in her beauty. Though she had none of the advantages in her youth that wealth and refined associations afford, yet her moral nature was so well nourished that dissipation in the mad whirl of social gaities, and lastly in the vortex of sensual vice, failed to destroy all the honorable instincts with which she had been endowed. She was a favorite, and in the exhausting effort to retain her pre-eminence as the star of her class, her health was broken, and she became the mistress of that inexorable master, consumption, whose touch is the kiss of death.

Act I. of the opera begins with a supper given at Violetta's house, with a preliminary scene which represents the fair hostess seated on a sofa in her drawing-room, with her physician and a number of friends, as the invited guests are arriving, among the earliest being Flora Bevoix, escorted by Marquis d'Obiguy, and Baron Duphol. As these three enter, Violetta rises to give them welcome, saying,

"Flora, be welcome, my friends, I salute ye.
This night let all be mirthful and gay.
Naught so bright as when wine cups are flashing."

Observing the sickly pallor of their hostess' cheeks, the trembling step, and feeble hand, Flora and the Marquis anxiously ask if she has health for such enjoyment, to which Violetta, assuming a cheerfulness which she does not feel, replies,

"Why ask me? It is in pleasure alone that I exist, and it is the only physician that can cure."

At this juncture Gaston, a mutual friend, enters with Alfred Germont, whom he introduces as a gentleman who is loyal in love as in honor, who confesses to being one of the many admirers of Violetta, and who desires to pay his devotions. The stricken woman is flattered by this admission, and extending her hand, which Alfred kisses, assures him of a cordial welcome.

When supper is served, Violetta takes her seat between Alfred and Gaston, while Flora is placed between the Marquis and the Baron, and this convenient arrangement permits of Gaston talking in a low and confidential tone to Violetta, in which he

"Seize we the swift-winged hours.
Let joy crown the cup with flowers."

declares the burning love that Alfred bears for her, and when she would question Gaston's words by appeal to Alfred himself, he fervently vows his passion. The Baron has seen Violetta's lover, and these confidences arouse his jealousy, which he expresses to Flora, but represses an exhibition of his anger at her caution. The company become merry under the influence of jest and wine, until Gaston requests the Baron to sing "a mirth-stirring ditty," when with a frown of impatience he positively refuses. A like request is then made of Alfred, who, though at first mildly protesting, responds, at the wish of Violetta, with a drinking song.

> "Where beauty, where beauty and mirth are beckoning,
> Seize we the swift-winged hours;
> Let joy, let joy crown the cup with flowers.
> And life's a dream of bliss." etc.

Under the excitement evoked by the song, Violetta rises and sings a complementary verse, and when the chorus finishes, Alfred and Violetta declare their love in a duet, during which music is heard in another room. Interest in this new diversion is immediately manifested, and Violetta undertakes to lead the party to the place whence the music proceeds, but advancing a few steps her weakness compels her to pause, and confessing a momentary faintness, to anxious inquiries, she bids her guests proceed alone, which all obey save Alfred. The two are thus left alone and thereby opportunity is given the ardent lover to caution her against wearing out her life in such midnight revels, and to express the intensity of his passion. She professes for a while to doubt his sincerity, appreciating her unworthiness of the devotion which he vows, and to his protestations she finally, in a sacrificial spirit, declares.

> "If this is true, fly from me; friendship is all I offer
> I know not such devotion; I live for joy and liberty.
> Friends will I have for pleasure;
> If such thou dost not treasure, erase me from thy heart.
> Farewell, thou soon wilt forget me."

Alfred chides her as being incapable of loving, whereat she begs him to say no more, but to leave her. When he would obey she takes a flower from her breast, and giving it to him asks him to return it to her when 'tis faded. At this permission, which she gives him to meet her again, Alfred is transported with joy, and, breathing again his undying love, farewell is spoken. The company reappear, heated from dancing, and sing in chorus a parting song.

> "See, the morning sun is gleaming.
> Let us now depart from hence." etc.

Violetta now left alone, pours out her heart upon the altar of love in a solo of exquisite pathos:

> "No love of mortal yet hath moved thee;
> Oh, rapture I never knew of, to love a heart devoted!
> Shall I dare to disdain it, and choose the empty follies
> That now surround me." etc.

But in the midst of this delight, she suddenly calls to mind the depths to which she has socially descended, and believing that such joy as she has discovered is but an idle dream, she lapses into melancholy and resolves to give herself up to pleasure, feeling that no one can sincerely love a woman who is so fallen as she. While thus voicing her bitter thoughts, Alfred appears under her balcony to repeat his vows, and while he sings,

> "Love, thou art life and breath of all creation."

Violetta disappears and the curtain falls on Act I.

Act II. opens in a country house near Paris, to which Violetta has repaired with Alfred, and where for three months the couple have lived in a condition of supreme happiness. Alfred enters the house upon returning from a hunt, and, putting away his gun, renders a beautiful recitative that tells of his joy in the sweet consummation of his love with Violetta.

> "When we are parted, of life itself I m weary;
> Three months have nearly vanished
> Since my beloved Violetta left for my sake
> The world, its pleasures and splendors,
> The gay and brilliant circle where she,
> The star of beauty, enslaved the hearts of all,
> And here, contented with me to roam the meadows,
> She forgets all for me.
> Her gracious presence renews all my being
> In thee is cancell'd all dark
> Remembrance of a past distracted."

LA TRAVIATA

While thus recounting his happiness, Alfred is interrupted by the sudden entrance of Annina, Violetta's maid, who tells him that her mistress has expressed the wish that all her property be sold at once, as the expense of keeping a country house can no longer be supported, besides, many debtors are already importunate, and she has no other means to satisfy them. Alfred is much astonished and asks what amount is needed to discharge these obligations, to which Annina replies—though her mistress has forbid her to tell the source of her distress—"the sum of two thousand louis."

"I will then go away to Paris, but do not mention a word to your mistress. Go, go!" exclaims Alfred impatiently; and when again alone he reproaches himself for having been regardless of the expenditures made by Violetta, and for omitting to do the honorable part of a man, not to say lover, toward one who has sacrificed so much for his sake. He now resolves to redeem himself by going at once to Paris to obtain the money that is required to save Violetta's property from sale, determined that she shall not see him again until his honor is thus retrieved. At the exit of Alfred, Violetta enters with Annina, of whom she inquires, "Where is Alfred?" To which the maid answers that he has just gone to Paris to be absent until the following morning. When Violetta is expressing surprise at her lover's sudden departure, Joseph, her man-servant, enters with a letter which he hands to the worried woman, who seats herself at a table as the two servants pass out. The letter proves to be an invitation from her friend, Flora, to a ball that is to be given that evening, which Violetta, after reading, tosses carelessly upon the table with the remark, "She will wait for me in vain," for Violetta has eschewed all her social gaieties, has abandoned all her follies, in order to devote herself to the man she so dearly loves, in whom alone she has found the real pleasures and joys of life.

Joseph now reappears at the door to announce a stranger, whose visit, however, had been anticipated by a note which Violetta received during the morning. The visitor advances, with great dignity of manner, and asks,

"Is this Violetta Valery?"

And when she answers truly, the stranger declares himself to be Mons. Germont, "the father of the incautious madman whom you are luring to ruin."

Violetta rises and resents this rude speech by reminding Germont that she is beneath her own roof, and a woman, therefore she would leave him for his sake rather than for her own.

The instincts of a gentleman come to Germont to reprove him for his offensive words, and by assuming a more respectful manner he prevails upon her to remain and listen to his proposals. Germont accuses Violetta of receiving and squandering the wealth of Alfred, and when she declares the falsity of this charge, he asks,

"Whence, then, comes all this splendor that I see?"

To prove her statement that Alfred has given her nothing, Violetta hands Germont a paper, which is the pawnbroker's receipt for her furniture and jewels, and thus proving by a sale of all her worldly belongings that their support has come from her own purse, tells him that she has abandoned her former mode of living, has cancelled the past and devoted herself to Alfred, for whom her love is so great that heaven has blotted out her sin through the sincerity of her repentance.

"Oh, yes," responds Germont, "your heart is noble, and from it I will therefore ask a great concession."

Violetta foresees in this request some impending calamity, some dreadful sacrifice, a doom to her happy hopes, but she listens. Germont tells her the story of his own domestic afflictions, which have been caused by the scandal of Alfred's connection with her, that he is the father of two children, one of whom is a beautiful daughter, both loving and loved, in whom his fondest hopes are centred, who is fair as a rose in Paradise, but whose life is being blasted, who is fading like a flower with broken stem, for she cannot be wedded while Alfred is in the thrall of a woman such as she.

Thinking that she understands the meaning of his complaint, Violetta is ready to make the sacrifice of a parting from Alfred until his sister's marriage, but Germont tells her that the happiness of himself and daughter, and of Alfred as

well, can be obtained only by her consent to a complete and final separation, and a renouncement of her love! To this pleading of the father Violetta wails her answer,

"the heaven apeth Tis speaks through me To turn my loved ones' fate."

— Ah, no! Never! Ah, you know not how I love him.
How I treasure naught above him.
Neither father, friend nor brother lives to comfort or to guide me,
But to love me and protect me there is none but only he.
Ah, you know not, o'er my life-spring
Deadly sickness is impending.
Daily, hourly, death hovers o'er me;
No, I cannot part from Alfred!
What you ask, Oh, my aching spirit cannot bear it,
Rather, Oh, rather than part, Oh, let me die!"

Germont has some compassion for the anguished woman, but as his own honor and happiness are so deeply involved, he attempts to persuade and to console Violetta by reminding her that men's hearts are changeable; that the ardor of Alfred's love will cool toward her when he realizes the gulf between them; that it were better to make a sacrifice now than to bow later before the realization of delusive dreams. Perceiving that she wavers in her resolution, Germont supplicates by this moving speech,

— But thou canst be my children's angel, bearing sweet comfort;
Violetta, Oh, bethink thee well, resolve ere 'tis too late;
'Tis heaven itself that speaks through me
To turn my loved ones' fate."

Unable to resist such a pathetic plea, and realizing the social infamy which must ever attach to her, and which Alfred must share if the alliance continue, she at length consents to sacrifice her hopes, her life, to the pleading father and the happiness of his innocent daughter, and thus she answers, out of the depths of her agony,

— Say to thy daughter, guarded and cherished,
That one unhappy heart for her hath perished;
One single hope had she, only one single hope e'er did bless her,
That blessed hope she hath now sacrificed for her sake.

The pity of Germont is now fully excited, and he confesses,

— Bitter, bitter sorrow speaks in thy words.
Bitter, bitter sorrow speaks in thy accents;
Great is thy anguish, great thy devotion.
And while I ask the boon, I sorrow for thee;
Thy noble heart heaven will never forsake."

Violetta asks Germont to advise her how she shall separate from Alfred, for if she should tell him she does not love him, he will not believe her, and if she should leave him he will follow, but that she will nevertheless pass through the agony of a trial. She then asks Germont to embrace her as a daughter, promising that Alfred shall soon be restored to him, and to wait in the garden until he shall meet him there. As she is about to write a note of renunciation, Germont says, "Generous damsel, how can I ever repay thy goodness?"

To which expression of gratitude she replies,

— No need! 'tis death alone can give me rest;
But, Oh! do not let him curse me,
But let his tender memory enshrine my name unhappy,
May he be spared the anguish that rends my soul tormented
But may he know for him alone I breathed my latest sigh."

Germont would stay to console Violetta with assurances of great reward for the sacrifice, but she embraces and begs him to go, with which request he complies by passing into the garden, whereupon Violetta prepares to write the parting letter, and calling Annina, orders her to deliver it at once to Alfred. But while she is writing, Alfred enters, and seeing an unfinished note before her, asks to whom she is writing. Violetta is greatly embarrassed, which Alfred quickly relieves by telling her he is aware of his father's visit, but that though he had left an angry letter he is sure his father will love her when he sees her.

With great agitation Violetta implores Alfred to let her go hence, and to meet his father alone; that it were better he should not find them together, for when his father shall hear him tell how great is their love he will not ask them to part, and blissful moments may yet be theirs

"Why, then, Jo you weep?" asks Alfred.

"My heart has need of tears to calm it," she answers. To reassure him she says.

> "I can be calm now. 'Tis over. I am smiling.
> I'll be there 'mongst the flowers.
> Near when you call me, always near to thee.
> Alfred. Oh love me, love me as I do thee!
> How fare thee - well"

And thus parting from him, she retires hastily into the garden, and Alfred seats himself with an open book to await the coming of his father. Joseph now enters, excitedly, and informs Alfred that Violetta and Annina have suddenly taken coach for Paris, but Alfred is not alarmed, believing that Violetta has gone to make a sale of her belongings, which, however, will be prevented by Annina, to whom he has given instructions that will avoid the sacrifice. Alfred sees some one in the garden, and as he is about to go out to inquire whom it may be, a commissioner appears at the door to tell him the visitor is Mons. Germont, at the same time delivering into his hands a letter, which, to his surprise, he discovers to be from Violetta, and upon opening reads these cruel words,

"When, Alfred, you will receive these lines, we're sundered."

With a cry of anguish he is about to fall, but is caught in his father's arms, who tries in vain to console him by saying,

"Despair not! My son, take comfort! Ah, cease from weeping; return unto thy father, his pride and his solace."

But Alfred repulses this effort to console, and declares he will have vengeance, for he believes that it is through the machinations of Duphol that Violetta has been induced to thus abandon him. Seeing the letter from Flora lying upon the table, Alfred feverishly reads it, and then suddenly concluding that Violetta has gone to the party announced for that evening, he rushes out distractedly for Flora's home, followed by his father, who insists upon accompanying him, to prevent his doing some rash thing

The next scene represents a richly furnished apartment in Flora's mansion, in which are gathered the hostess, Marquis d'Obigny, Doctor Crenvil, and other guests. Flora speaks with the Marquis and tells him she expects the presence of Alfred and Violetta, but the Marquis interrupts to ask.

> "Why, have you not heard the news, then?
> That Alfred and she are disunited?
> If she comes 'twill be with the Baron."

The conversation is interrupted by the entrance of maskers disguised as Gypsies, one of whom reads the hand of Flora, and then scans the palm of the Marquis, telling the former that she shall have a rival, and the latter that his love is inconstant, by which means seeds of jealousy are sown in the mind of Flora, and the Marquis attempts in vain to disquiet her forebodings. Gaston and others, in the guise of Matadors and Picadors, now rush in and sing of their prowess in the arena and their conquests of love, concluding with a chorus by all.

> "Come and tempt us Fortune's chances.
> See, the fickle goddess smiles.
> Play alone the heart entrances.
> Play our file with bliss beguiles."

The company remove their masks, and some of the gentlemen begin to play at the gaming tables that are provided, when at this juncture Alfred appears. Flora anxiously asks him about Violetta, but he frowns and disdainfully declares he knows nothing of her. The answer is heard by all present, who exhibit their surprise by looks and speech, but seek to divert him from any sad reflections by inquiring,

"What are you indeed parted? Wondrous!
Come, then, let us play at cards."

Alfred accepts the banter, and goes with Gaston and others to the table, upon which he places his money. While they are thus engaged, Violetta enters, upon the arm of the Baron, at sight of whom Alfred's suspicions are confirmed, and his rage is intense, but he restrains himself with a show of indifference. Violetta has not expected to meet Alfred in this place, and she trembles with anxiety and irresolution at the sight of him; perceiving her agitation the Baron admonishes,

"Take care, with this intruder a word you must not interchange."

Flora comes to the rescue of Violetta by inviting her to sit on the sofa, where she seeks to console her and to learn the cause of the rupture between her and Alfred. During this side-conversation Alfred is playing high stakes and invariably winning. He remarks,

"They say mischance in loving marks good success in gaming."

"Yes, fortune smiles upon me,
And all my golden treasure,
On my return I'll shower
In my abode of pleasure."

"All alone?" interrupts Flora.

"No! no!" Alfred answers, "with one who erewhile has shared my pastimes, and since left me."

A sigh escapes Violetta.

Gaston implores Alfred to spare Violetta, and the Baron expresses his anger, but is restrained by Violetta, who commands forbearance under threat of leaving him. But Alfred has heard the first words of the Baron, and asks if he had called? The Baron answers ironically, saying,

"Such is your wondrous fortune that I to play with you am tempted."

Alfred eagerly accepts the challenge, and the play begins. The stakes are first for one hundred louis ($400), which Alfred wins, and then the wagers are doubled, but without changing the result, until the Baron has lost to his antagonist all the money upon his person.

Supper is now announced, and the guests go out, leaving Alfred and the Baron behind, at which Violetta is distracted with fear, and exclaims, aside,

"What will betide? Oh, I must part them!
Forsake me not; Oh, Heaven! forsake me not!"

Alfred asks the Baron if he will continue the game, but his beaten rival answers

"To-night it is concluded, another time I'll take revenge."

"At any game you please, sir," is Alfred's taunting reply, and the two pass out.

A moment later Violetta re-enters, betraying great agitation, having signaled Alfred to follow, which he is prompt to obey, and the distracted lovers are now alone for a painful interview. Violetta begs him to leave the place, where he is surrounded by naught but perils, which admonishment Alfred interprets as a desire upon her part to rid herself of his presence that she may the more unreservedly enjoy the company of the Baron. When he accuses her of such base purpose, she declares it is not so, but lest fear lest the Baron should challenge him to a duel, saying,

"But if he should be the slayer!
Ah! bethink thee, I implore thee,
'Tis for that alone I tremble.

Alfred promises to leave the place if she will follow, but when she refuses by declaring that she cannot, he asks what power prevents, to which she replies,

"Oh, me, unhappy! Go, forget me and my sorrow,
I conjure thee, for remember that a fatal oath compels me to refuse thee."

LA TRAVIATA

Alfred presses her for more specific reason, to know to whom she owes submission, and finally asks if it is to Duphol? The question is like a dagger struck at her heart, but even in her agony she still continues her sublime sacrifice by answering.

"Yes."

"Then you love him?"

"Alas!" answers the anguished woman, "I love him."

In all the fury of a jealous-maddened lover, Alfred rushes to the door and shouts to the company within, "Come out and hear!" and as the guests run in to discover the cause of this furious outbreak, he points to Violetta, who, overwhelmed with grief, leans upon a table to support herself, while he hurls this denunciation upon her:

> "Twas upon me this creature vile lavished her whole possessions.
> I, wretched, blinded, credulous, trusted her base professions.
> All I accepted, loving her,
> But since I have unmasked her,
> I call on you to witness.
> Friends, that I have paid her now."

At the conclusion of this impassioned accusation, he throws the money he has won of Duphol at the feet of Violetta, who falls in a faint. The whole company resent this violent outburst from Alfred, to which Germont, his father, though feeling the pangs of wounded conscience, adds an execration:

> "Tis shame to manhood to insult a woman;
> Of odious harshness thou hast been guilty;
> The son I cherished is lost forever.
> I must renounce thee; my child thou art no more."

Alfred is tormented with conflicting emotions, crying,

> "While I with hatred rash would pursue her,
> Her sweet remembrance still I adore!"

The guests all condole with Violetta by words of loving encouragement, and Germont, aside, confesses his own cruelty for severing a couple who could love so devotedly, while the Baron resents the insult thus given to Violetta by warning Alfred of his purpose to seek revenge at their next meeting.

With a faint and plaintive voice, Violetta answers this fierce malediction of her lover by a tender tribute that proclaims the depths of her affections:

> "Oh, Alfred! Alfred! alas thou knowest not how true and tenderly
> This heart hath loved thee: with faith undaunted,
> When trials proved thee, I braved thy scorning — but that is o'er
> But time will show thee, alas, too surely,
> How thou hast wronged one who loved thee purely.
> That on that day full remorse may spare thee.
> I Heaven will implore! Oh, my love, though thou forget,
> Although thou forget me, I am thine evermore!"

This scene concludes Act II.

Scene I. of Act III. shows Violetta's chamber, and a bed with curtains half-drawn, upon which she is lying, while a table containing a decanter of water, a glass and medicines, indicate the illness of the room's occupant. A fire is burning in a grate, before which Annina is seated, asleep from weary watching. Violetta awakens and calls her maid, who, rousing herself, in obedience to her mistress' command, opens a window that looks out upon the street and announces the approach of the doctor. Violetta tries to rise from her bed, but her weakness is such that she requires assistance, which Annina renders and leads her to a sofa as the doctor enters. Feeling the sufferer's pulse, he asks if she is not better, to which Violetta answers.

> "Yes, spite of faintness, for my mind is tranquil
> A heavenly consolation hath dawned upon me;
> Ah! naught else but prayer can relieve my spirit"

LA TRAVIATA

The doctor bids her be of good courage, for her illness will soon be conquered, and, pressing her hand, says good-bye till evening. As he goes out, Annina follows to ask in confidence if indeed her mistress is better, to which the physician replies, "It can be but a few hours ere all is over."

Annina re-enters the room and tries to cheer the patient, but Violetta realizes that death is near at hand, and now gives her last instructions:

"How much money is in my drawer?" she asks, and being told that only twenty louis remain, Violetta requests her to give half the sum to the needy and go inquire if a letter has come. When Annina goes out of the room, Violetta draws a letter from her bosom, which she reads, as follows:

> "You have kept your promise — the duel took place —
> The Baron was wounded, but he is recovering
> Alfred is in a foreign land ;
> He will return to implore your pardon.
> I, too, shall come. Take care of your health,
> And trust to a happy future.
> — George Germont (father of Alfred)."

Pale, almost exhausted, suffering in both heart and body, an object of extreme compassion, by great effort Violetta rises, saying,

"It is late! I've trusted and waited, but, alas, he comes not!"

Looking at her faded face in the mirror, in a hollow voice she continues her soliloquy,

> "Oh! can I be so altered? But the doctor said I should soon recover.
> Oh, but this faintness tells plainly all is hopeless!
> Forever I must leave thee,
> Thou fair world of sorrow, my roses all faded.
> The hope that sustained me, alas, now hath perished ;
> Vain are the dreams that so fondly I cherished.
> I am weary of life.
> But yonder, my errors may yet be forgiven :
> If men are relentless, there's mercy in heaven."

A chorus of revelers is heard outside, and Annina reappears with cheerful countenance to tell her mistress a piece of good news, an unexpected pleasure. Violetta anticipates that it is Alfred's return which Annina is thus preparing to announce, and the next moment her happy hope is realized, for Alfred enters and rushes into the arms of the woman who has sacrificed her life to secure the happiness of Germont and his daughter. Alfred has been told by his father of all that Violetta has sacrificed, and he has returned at this late hour to implore a pardon, which she now has barely the strength to grant, and give reassurance of her changeless devotion. The supreme hour of his affliction, the grief that follows realization of a wrong which ebbing life prevents full correction, bursts with awful suddenness upon the now deeply anguished lover, who with racking conscience and breaking heart cries pityingly and disconsolate,

> "Oh, my Violetta, my love, my own beloved Violetta!
> Oh, love, forgive me for what thou hast suffered."

Feebly she interrupts Alfred's pleadings of distress with sweet pledges of forgiveness, gasping for breath to voice her utterance. "'Tis all forgot now in thy returning."

> "Oh, by this beating heart, learn how I love thee!
> No power in heaven or earth from thee
> Shall move me."

And thus the two, who have been deceived and deceiving, who have suffered torments that only broken hearts can feel, pledge anew their vows of devotion, and voice in tenderest accents the happiness that has swept them into Paradise upon a wave of joy. But the delight over this reunion proves too much for her endurance, and Violetta sinks upon a couch, as Annina, Germont and the doctor enter. Germont has come to take Violetta to his heart as a recompense for the noble sacrifices she has made, as an atonement for the heart-breaks he has caused, and tells her,

"Now I have come to claim thee, generous heart, to be my daughter."

LA TRAVIATA.

"Alas, too late to save me," Violetta feebly utters, while she embraces Germont, who, perceiving at this moment that she is dying, now shares with Alfred his bitterness, sorrow and remorse, exclaiming,

> "No more, my son, no more;
> Do not rend my heart with unavailing anguish;
> 'Tis as lightning from heaven, her gentle accents.
> Ill advised my precautions!
> Too late I feel it, I've foully wronged her."

Violetta rallies with a last effort to prove her love and pardon, and taking from a casket a medallion picture, speaks with last failing voice:

> "Come, draw nearer, and hear me;
> Oh, how I love thee!
> Alfred, receive this parting gift.
> The form of one who loved thee;
> When Heaven has hence removed me,
> My image 'twill recall."

Alfred, overwhelmed with grief, pours out his passion in a piercing wail, declaring she shall not die and that death itself shall not separate them. She tries to console him, and tells him if hereafter he shall meet a gentle maid, holy and pure and tender, if she her heart surrender, that he shall make such an one his wife; that he shall give her this token (the picture) and feel that " one in yonder shining sky prayeth for her, for thee."

Annina, Germont and the doctor express the depth of their sorrow and think her dead, but Violetta opens her eyes and speaks again:

> "The deadly pain that conquered me,
> And the faintness are gone.
> My pulses are beating.
> Here within I feel renewing life!
> Oh! I feel my life returning!
> What rapture!"

But it is only a heavenly dream, the spirit leaving its shattered tenement, a glorious vision that only the closing eye may see, and the soul may feel, when it gazes upon the no longer useful body, for with the word "rapture" upon her lips she falls back upon the sofa—dead.

Alfred calls to her, but to his despairing cry there is no answer; the sudden joy, the scene, the life of the martyr to love is ended.

A SKETCH OF RICHARD WAGNER.

WHATEVER be the claims of critics, whether inspired by jealousy or prompted by serious judgment, the fact must remain unquestioned and conspicuous that, so far at least as modern opera is concerned, Richard Wagner is the most prominent of the great composers; I may say, indeed, he is the most renowned author, creator and exponent of that form of lyric drama that has exerted the largest influence upon contemporary music and its devotees, whose influence, though for a while restricted and decried, is now rapidly embracing the masses.

Wagner, whose name was originally William Richard, was born in Leipsic, May 22, 1813, the son of a poor but honest man, whose sole distinction was that of police actuary, and who died when Richard was a babe scarcely six months old. His mother was illy prepared to battle with the hardships which were thus imposed upon her, but she was both heroic and devoted, and struggled most industriously to provide advantages for her two children, Richard and Rosalie. She was unable to give her son a finished education, but the boy mastered many of his natural obstacles by aptitude and application, for when only twelve years of age he wrote two plays of no inconsiderable merit, which in fact exhibited unusual maturity of thought and afforded promise of a brilliant attainment. Three years later he was so deeply impressed by hearing a rendition of Beethoven's symphonies that he resolved to become a musician, and forthwith began a systematic study of the art under Theodore Weinlig, even while continuing as a student at the Leipsic University. So rapid was his advancement that at the age of seventeen Richard submitted a composition, of a symphony character, that received the highest praise from his teacher. At the age of twenty he wrote another symphony, which was produced at a concert in Leipsic, and in the same year he composed a romantic opera entitled "The Fairies." This piece can hardly be called an original composition, made up as it was so largely from Weber and Marschner, but considering the age and studies of the author, a considerable measure of credit is due him, for it manifests the acuteness of his comprehension of the greatest musicians of his time and his conception of situations that produce the most powerful effects. It should be noted also that Wagner not only wrote the music, adapted though it may be, but the libretto also, and that he was the author of the words, music and score of every opera he composed. Thus Wagner is shown to be poet, litterateur, and musician, in all of which branches he exhibits remarkable proficiency, a versatility of accomplishments which is exceeding rare.

Wagner never saw his first opera, "The Fairies," staged but in 1868, five years after his death, it was presented in Munich and met with such favor as to justify its frequent representation since.

In 1834 Wagner composed his second opera, "Das Liebesverbot," ("Interdicted Love") founded upon Shakespeare's "Measure for Measure," which had only a single performance, at Magdeburg. At this time he was musical director of the theatre at that place, and so great was his mortification over the failure of the opera that he resigned his position in Magdeburg and went to Konigsberg, where he secured a similar place, and where in 1836 he married. Early in 1837 he moved to Riga to assume the directorship of music at the theatre of that city. In 1838, while living in Riga, Wagner composed "Rienzi," which he designed particularly for a Paris presentation, with the hope and belief that it would serve the beneficent purpose of establishing him in the affections of the Parisians, whose appreciation of opera, at the time, was greater than that of any other people. But his ambition was not yet to be fulfilled, for upon reaching Paris, in 1839, almost perishing in a shipwreck on the way, he found influence lacking to secure a production of his opera there, and his means being small he

RICHARD WAGNER

was compelled to resort for a while to song writing for a music publisher named Maurice Schlesinger. But he presently came to know Meyerbeer, the composer, and with this extension of his acquaintance among other self-expatriated Germans

A SKETCH OF RICHARD WAGNER

in the French capital, he was not long in securing artistic recognition. His songs, while full of melody, were not very popular, because of the often offensive and nearly always eccentric character of the verses, but this latter was so far excused by those who perceived the genius latent in his music that he secured a commission to write an overture for the Concert Association of Paris. The result of this labor was "Faust," which after a single rehearsal was abandoned on account of the same objections which had been conspicuous in his songs. This rejection of a composition upon which he had set his whole store of dependence was a hard blow, not only to his ambition but to his very existence, for he thus became reduced to the sorest straits, which he admits in his writings thus. "Manifold difficulties and very bitter want encompassed my life at this period."

BIRTHPLACE OF WAGNER

Though through this season of pecuniary distress Wagner wrote ballads of more or less questionable character, he continued his nobler work in the field of Grand Opera. He not only persisted in the re-writing of "Rienzi" and preparing, in the minutest detail, the whole instrumental embellishments, but contributed many articles on German music to the *Paris Musical Gazette*. In addition to all this work he set about the composition of the "Flying Dutchman," which he completed in the short period of seven weeks, and sent the score to his friend Meyerbeer, who was then in Berlin, where it was subsequently produced. But with all his efforts he was unable to secure a representation of "Rienzi" in Paris, and at length, thoroughly despairing of accomplishing his ambitious purposes at the French capital, in 1842 he went to Dresden, where in October of the same year he had the infinite satisfaction of obtaining the encouragement he had so long sought for in vain by inducing a magnificent production of "Rienzi." Its success was as immediate as it was pronounced. Dresden audiences were infatuated, nor were popular acclamations his only reward, for as a national recognition of his genius the Emperor conferred upon him the distinguished order of the Red Eagle, and he was pressed to accept the position of chapel master at the Dresden Opera House. His fame became thus as secure as it was great, though suddenly acquired, and henceforth he rose a sun amid the stellary galaxy of composers.

Wagner wrote and saw produced his "Tannhäuser" in 1845, but after two performances it was withdrawn for lack of appreciation. Undismayed by this, however, he set about the composition of "Lohengrin," but when preparation for its production was about completed, in 1849, a revolutionary outbreak occurred in Saxony, which prevented for the time a realization of his intentions. Most unfortunately for his interests as a composer, Wagner had so far identified himself with the radical party so as to be regarded as a leader, and when the uprising was suppressed he was compelled to seek safety by a flight to Zurich. Here he renewed his operatic labors, and during the nine years of his residence in Zurich, most of which time he was director of the orchestra, he composed "Tristan and Isolde," and a greater part of his tetralogy, or the four master operas founded upon the legends of the Nibelungenlied.

Wagner was fortunate in many ways after his escape from Dresden, not the least of which was a friendship which he formed with Franz Liszt, which was especially valuable to him, for Liszt was one of the most popular and influential men of his day, and deservedly so as a man and as a composer. Through Liszt's efforts "Lohengrin" was brought out at Weimar in August, 1850, following which successful presentation others of Wagner's operas were staged in a splendid manner in the same city.

In the latter part of 1859 Wagner received a political pardon from the King of Saxony, and he was induced soon after to take up his residence at Munich, where he quickly became a favorite of Louis II., King of Bavaria, whose munificent patronage enabled him to carry into effect his most ambitious plans. It was by Louis' assistance that "Tristan and Isolde" was given its initial representation in Munich in 1865, under Von Bulow's immediate direction, followed by "The Master-singers of Nuremberg," in 1868, "The Rheingold," in 1869, "The Valkyrie" and "Siegfried," in 1870, and "Gotterdammerung" ("Dusk of the Gods"), in 1871.

In 1870 Wagner married his second wife, Cosima, a daughter of Liszt, who had been divorced from Von Bulow in 1869, who survives at this writing and devotes her means and energies to the advancement of the school of opera which her world-famous husband created and established at Bayreuth. Directly after his second marriage, Wagner conceived the rather extravagant yet praiseworthy idea of building a theatre which should be devoted to representations of his operas, a scheme which King Louis so substantially advanced that a location was decided upon in 1871, and on May 22, 1872, the foundation stone of the theatre was laid in the isolated and small city of Bayreuth, in north Bavaria. The work of construction was delayed, however, because of an insufficiency of funds, so that it was not until the summer of 1876 that the theatre was completed. The pianoforte rehearsals of what Wagner called the "Festival Stage Play" were given in the unfinished building in 1875, so that when the work of construction was ended preparations were at the same time fully effected for the performance of the four operas, or tetralogy, which were produced with such a bewildering magnificence of mechanical, orchestral, and dramatic effect that the musical world was moved to an ecstasy which has not yet subsided. Bayreuth has, by reason of the annual Wagnerian festivals, which have ever since continued, become a shrine for music-loving devotees, and though somewhat inconvenient to reach, the town itself has acquired great fame, and on the occasions when Wagner's operas are represented there its temporary population is many thousands, comprising visitors from every part of the civilized world.

WAGNER'S VILLA, BAYREUTH.

I visited the town in July, 1897, during the music festival of that year, and was filled with amazement at the miserable inconveniences and poverty-appearance of the place, and my wonderment at Wagner's selection may never cease. The only recommendation that Bayreuth possesses is its isolation, where other attractions are so few that the interest of visitors may not be diverted from the performances, but this benefit is impaired by the necessity of those who would enjoy the theatre seeking lodgings at Nuremberg, thirty miles distant, where the hotels are excellent.

Wagner has the distinction of being not only the most famous composer, but also of having been a man of great literary ability as well, for while he was author of operas that make his name illustrious, he was also an industrious and accomplished writer—though chiefly on subjects appertaining to music—whose works 'ave a claim, upon those at least who are especially interested in the history of music, next in importance to his operas themselves.

Wagner's last composition was "Parsifal," which is a religious drama, connected with myths of the Holy Grail, to which "Lohengrin" belongs. "Parsifal" was begun in 1859, but it was not completed until 1882, during the author's sojourn at Palermo, and only three months before its first production at Bayreuth. Though written when Wagner was far advanced in years, competent critics have pronounced it the grandest of his several sublime and imperishable creations. And there is an impressive, if not a significant, foreshadowing in the theme and treatment of "Parsifal," which it were not irreverent to compare to the song of the dying swan,—most melodious in its expiring notes. The sweet singer may have caught a glimpse of the heavenly vision and longed to direct the celestial choir; his heart had inclined

WAGNER THEATRE, BAYREUTH.

toward those consolements that minister no longer to worldly ambitions, and which lift the soul to delightful contemplations of the beauties and joys that are to be found nowhere save in the land of the ineffable. And so let us believe, for, seven months after "Parsifal" was completed, while spending a winter season in Venice, the Great Wagner surrendered forever both pen and baton (February 13, 1883), and joined the immortal choir invisible, amid the lamentations of the world.

Tannhäuser

(AFTER THE ORIGINAL PAINTING BY WILLIAM DE LEFTWICH DODGE)

TANNHAUSER—"*Holy Saint Elizabeth, oh, pray for me!*"

ACT III.—LAST SCENE.

TANNHÄUSER.

By Richard Wagner.

TANNHÄUSER belongs to what may be called mediæval mythology, embodying, as the story does, a legend that strangely combines religion of the Middle Ages with the passions of love, jealousy, and venal sin, which form the most common basis of tales that move to compassion and excite the strongest impulses of the human heart. Many strange, even remarkable, superstitions prevailed throughout Europe during that transition period when Protestantism was obtaining a firm footing and extending its influence, which became more or less powerful factors in the fierce rivalry precipitated upon Catholicism by Luther's adherents. It will be remembered that after Luther's return to Wittenberg, following his arraignment before the august—the royal and the ecclesiastical —Diet at Worms, he lodged in the Castle of Wartburg, in Thuringia, where he remained for ten months translating the New Testament. It is easy to understand how the bitterness of religious antagonism, in all the variable moods and outbursts of which such uncompromising jealousies of faiths are capable, brought forth myth as well as argument, and how missionaries would use both to influence the ignorant of the time. And especially would we expect the incitement of superstition to be strong in Thuringia, where the leader of Papal opposition had made his home and issued what many declared to be the most heretical edicts. Tannhäuser fully meets this expectation in plot, period, and place.

The myth upon which the story of Tannhäuser and Venus is founded antedates the Middle Ages, but it was little known until its versification by Tieck. The Teutonic religion, which was built up, so to speak, upon the miraculous and the marvelous, represented Holda, a goddess corresponding to the Latin Venus, as occupying a cavern in a mountain called the Horselberg, which is in Thuringia, a central region of Germany, with the Hartz mountains on the north and the Thuringian forests on the south. This district, almost from time immemorial, has been invested with strange superstitions, concerning gods of war and spirits of passion, several of which have been utilized by Wagner for operatic dramatization, and by Goethe and Tieck for poetical recital. The modernization, so to speak, of one of these legends, so as to associate it with the missionary zeal of the Middle Ages, was Wagner's work in his lyrical treatments of Tannhäuser, which he accomplished without offence to any faith or tradition, and to the delight of the opera-loving world.

It was represented, and devoutly believed, in the long ago, that Holda, or Venus, as we prefer to call her, made her residence in the enchanted cave of the Horselberg, rather than in some castle of the skies, in order that she might be near the haunts of men and thus the better ply her seductive arts for their destruction. She was regarded as a kind of feminine Mephisto, appearing in the most fascinating disguises, and granting the most affective favors to such as came within her influence, who were thus induced to indulge such sensual vices as would alienate the soul from all thoughts of heaven or the goodness of God.

Tannhäuser was the most famous of Thuringian minstrels, who, like Orpheus, had won so many prizes at musical tournaments that his pre-eminence was acknowledged, and he became the ideal of many a girl's heart, the fairest and most devoted of whom was Elizabeth,—daughter of the Landgrave prince of the Empire of Thuringia,—who died of unrequited love, as the story reveals.

The first scene of the opera is one of extraordinary beauty, representing in a hazy softness of exquisite colors, revealed by a diffusion of opalescent light, the mystic, eldouranion cavern of Venus, into which Tannhäuser has been beguiled by the beautiful goddess, who strives to excite his admiration by ravishing displays of her charms and to intoxicate his sensual senses by presenting before his wearied eyes

The Temptation of Tannhäuser.

a disporting company of nymphs and bacchantes, who dance to the measures of voluptuous strains, and pose before him in seductive attitudes. Tannhäuser has been a devotee in the charmed grotto for more than a year, and the caresses and diversions which Venus all this while has used to steep his soul with illicit gratification no longer avail her purposes, for the pleasure has begun to cloy, and the desire that possesses him now is to revisit the scenes of his youth, to look again upon the faces of his friends, to mingle with those who were once his companions, to dwell among mortals, where his minstrelsy shall awaken noble aspirations, and to look into the face of a woman whose love may redeem him from the shame to which he has fallen as a guilty captive of the lascivious goddess.

Venus is angered by his longing for liberty, nor is she moved by the tenderness of his appeal, and fiercely replies, "Traitor! Beware. Serpent heart ungrateful!"

Tannhäuser, in dread, and yet with some compunction for his inappreciation of the favors she has heaped upon him, the Cyprian blandishments with which he has so long been beguiled, uses sweet speech of persuasion and devotion, saying,

"But reft of thy sweet presence joy itself is hateful;
Yet fate compels me — 'tis for liberty I sigh."

Venus then renews her suppliant yearnings for his love, promising an immortality of bliss if he will remain the hero of her heart, to share the pleasures of her bower, to live with her in a revel and intoxication of sensual happiness that shall have no end. To which Tannhäuser makes answer:

"While I have life, my harp shall praise thee:
No other thing shall e'er my song inspire.
  * * * * * *
The fire thou kindled in my soul,
An altar flame shall burn for thee alone.
And yet for earth I'm yearning;
'Tis freedom I must win, or die,
For liberty I can everything defy;
Oh, queen, beloved goddess, let me fly!"

Enraged by his persistence, stung by jealousy at a rejection of her inducements, and maddened by his desire to abandon her, she turns upon him with this malediction:

"Then go. Oh, traitor heart! Away,
Thou madman, I will not detain thee.
Go! But thy longing shall be thy doom.
Go forth, thou madman!
Seek elsewhere for joy, but seek in vain,
Never to thee will heaven open,
Return then, if there is no hope."

Tannhäuser obtains the liberty for which he sighs, for Venus waves her hand and on the instant the grotto and all its voluptuous occupants dissolve: the opalescent light grows warmer until soon the sun pours down its midday glare, revealing Tannhäuser upon a hillside near a

ELIZABETH.

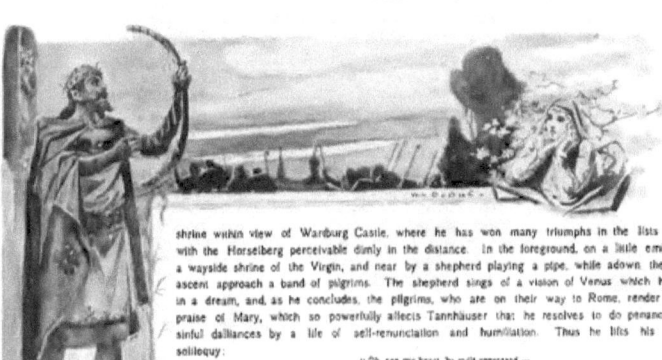

shrine within view of Wartburg Castle, where he has won many triumphs in the lists of song, with the Horselberg perceivable dimly in the distance. In the foreground, on a little eminence, is a wayside shrine of the Virgin, and near by a shepherd playing a pipe, while adown the winding ascent approach a band of pilgrims. The shepherd sings of a vision of Venus which he beheld in a dream, and, as he concludes, the pilgrims, who are on their way to Rome, render a choral praise of Mary, which so powerfully affects Tannhäuser that he resolves to do penance for his sinful dalliances by a life of self-renunciation and humiliation. Thus he lifts his voice in soliloquy:

"Oh, see my heart, by guilt oppressed,—
I faint, I sink beneath the burden.
Nor will I cease, nor will I rest,
Till heavenly mercy grants me pardon."

In the opening of the fourth scene the Landgrave, accompanied by a band of minstrels in hunting costume, are seen descending a forest path until they espy Tannhäuser, by the wayside, kneeling in prayer. They are surprised to find him, after so long an absence, and some of them cavalierly ask what his return signifies; whether he comes as friend or scornful foe; but Wolfram entertains no jealous suspicions and generously welcomes back the wandering minstrel, so long estranged. Thereupon all unite in expressions of welcome, but the Landgrave would have an explanation of his absence to which Tannhäuser replies by saying:

"In strange and distant realms I wandered far,
Where neither peace nor rest were ever found.
Ask not! At enmity I am with none,
We meet as friends—let me in peace depart."

The Landgrave is angered by Tannhäuser's refusal to tell the cause and story of his wanderings, and refuses him permission to depart, in which denial the others join, but when Tannhäuser declares that peace of mind can never be his again; that the past is closed to him forever, and that he is doomed to roam alone, unblest, the minstrels grow sympathetic and endeavor to persuade him to remain with them. In concert they picture the rest, relief, and joy which he may find by returning to his home and to the friends who will endeavor to lighten his griefs by tender ministrations. When these persuasions prove unavailing, Wolfram reminds Tannhäuser that here dwells Elizabeth, the sweet maid for whose hands the minstrels will contend, and for whose gracious favors the two are aspirants. By the mention of Elizabeth's name Tannhäuser is aroused from his heart oppression and betrays his love by saying:

"Elizabeth! Oh, rule of heaven,
That name adored once more I hear."

This reverent speech, for one whom all the minstrels worship, begets the gratitude and joy of those assembled who rejoice at the return of him who is greatest of the band. Perceiving the happy effects of his reminder Wolfram asks permission of the Landgrave to tell Tannhäuser of the prize he won at their last tournament of song, of the marvel his minstrelsy has wrought, in winning the heart of Elizabeth, the pure, the devout, the radiantly beautiful. The Landgrave is touched by this unselfish request, and being granted permission, Wolfram, with spirit, sings:

> "When for the palm in song we were contending,
> And oft thy conquering strain the wreath had won,
> Our songs anon thy victory suspending,
> One glorious prize was won by thee alone," etc.

The song finished, all unite in repeating their welcomes, and beseeching Tannhäuser to return to the minstrel brotherhood, which, with tenders of praise, and expressions of joy at the prospects of beholding Elizabeth, he appears to accept, as the curtain falls on the first act.

Act II.—Scene first shows the Hall of Minstrels in Wartburg Castle, in which Elizabeth appears greeting the place, and with plaintive voice she sings of the happiness that was hers when Tannhäuser's minstrelsy waked the echoes of the hall, and of her heart desolation when she was forsaken by the one whose song had taught her to love. The knowledge that he has returned, to enter the lists again, fills her soul with rapture which she thus voices:

> "But now the flame of hope is lighted,
> Thy vault shall ring with glorious war;
> For he whose strains my soul delighted
> No longer roams afar!"

Scene II.—Wolfram and Tannhäuser enter the hall and the former stops in deference to the feelings of his companion who advances and falls upon his knee before Elizabeth, who, startled, begs him to rise, as it is not proper they should meet here. Tannhäuser craves that he may stay a suppliant of her grace, but the coy maid insists that he shall rise, and though thankful that he has returned, desires to know where he has tarried so long, and what influence has caused him to come back. The interview is dramatic for its loving intensity, during which Tannhäuser expresses his contrition and devotion, but skilfully avoids explaining the enchantment that bound him as a slave to the seductive goddess. Elizabeth is content to receive his declaration that some marvel of heaven, working within his spirit, has directed him back to earth and to that holier shrine before which he is now a devotee. The two pledge their confidences, and pour out their thanksgiving in an exquisite duet.

> "Oh, blessed hour of meeting;
> Oh, blessed power of love."

and Wolfram joins in the refrain.

Scene III.—The Landgrave enters the Hall of Minstrels, and, greeting Elizabeth, asks if she has come to grace with her presence the contest that is about to take place, for since the departure of Tannhäuser she has not once appeared among the assemblage of minstrel knights. Elizabeth blushes with confusion, and to the Landgrave's request that she reveal her secret, she answers:

"Tell it, I cannot; read my eyes and know."

The Landgrave is too magnanimous to further seek to explore, by direct questioning, the love secret of his niece, and tells her that her treasured thoughts need not be spoken until such occasion as she may find it meet to declare them. This time, he feels, is near at hand, and thereupon informs her that,

> "The wondrous flame that song has kindled,
> This day shall brightly soar;
> Thy joy all hearts rejoicing,
> Shall on this day be crowned.
> What hath been sung shall spring to life for thee
> This day will see our nobles all assembled,
> To grace the solemn feast they now approach;
> None will be absent, since they know
> That once again thy hand the victor's wreath bestows."

A company of knights, nobles and minstrels enter, who sing,

"Hail, bright abode, where song the heart rejoices."

At the conclusion the Landgrave announces that a contest,—a singers' tourney,—is about to take place, the subject of which shall be "The Power of Love," and intimates that the hand of Elizabeth shall be the victor's prize. The full company of minstrels having gathered, and harps attuned, Wolfram is called upon to open the contest, permitted to select his theme, whereupon he pours forth an improvisation full of praise for the ideal of chastity, and a vision of purity. A chorus of nobles and ladies applaud the singer, but Tannhäuser interrupts to declare that such sentiments are not reflected by one who has known or tasted love; that Wolfram would embody an unapproached perfection, like the stars which were not made to be beloved. His ideal, he is bold enough to declare, is one who yields to soft caresses, framed in mortal mould that in his arms he may enfold, giving a joy that knows no measure, "for love's fulfillment is its pleasure."

These sensual ideals enrage the warrior knight Biteroll, who challenges Tannhäuser to mortal combat, which the nobles and ladies approve; but Tannhäuser disdains the defy of one whom he pronounces an idle boaster, and a grim wolf, who is incapable of feeling the divine passion. At this sally of insult the nobles are so offended that they draw their swords, but the Landgrave interposes, commanding that there shall be peace between them, and that Wolfram may conclude his apostrophe to chaste love.

When Tannhäuser is called he betrays the wildest exultation moved by the spirit of Venus which has entered his heart, and to her he indites his lay.

"Thou goddess of love, shall now inspire my measure,
In joyful strains thy praise be ever sung!
  *   *   *   *   *   *
Whose burning soul once hath with ardor embraced thee,
Can speak of love, none else its joys can prove.
Dull mortals, who of love have never tasted,
Go forth! Venus alone can show ye love."

Such sacrilege, such profanation of the pure, heavenly-descended aspiration and reflection of deity, creates great dismay among the ladies, all of whom, save Elizabeth, abruptly quit the hall, as the Landgrave pronounces a malediction upon Tannhäuser, and the knights and nobles rush upon him with drawn swords. But to their consternation Elizabeth rushes between, crying, "Stay your hands," begging pardon for her recreant, Venus-worshiping lover, in the name of Him who is merciful to the greatest sinner.

"Stand back, or pierce this bosom with your swords!
Death and its terrors cannot crush me
Like to the deadly wound that he hath struck me here."
  *   *   *   *   *   *
"Think not of me; he must be saved.
Ye would not rob his hope of heaven!"

When the Landgrave and nobles protest that a crime like his can ne'er be forgiven, and that her scorn were well deserved, Elizabeth defends in the name of our Saviour, and by thus defending exposes the secret of her boundless love, which confession wrings the heart of Tannhäuser with a sorrow and sense of wrong unutterable, so that he is able only to exclaim,

"Oh! lost, and forever."

The evil inspiration of Venus has been dissipated by the merciful and loving voice of the gentle maid, and the awful realization of his crime now breaks upon his comprehension, so that to the anathemas of the Landgrave and the nobles

TANNHAUSER

Tannhäuser is able to cry only for mercy, and offer prayer that his soul may be set free. They spurn and banish him, with reminders of how he has abused the sacred privileges of the Hall, but the Landgrave, more compassionate than the rest, and moved to pity by the anguish of his niece, tells Tannhäuser that one way is left by which he may escape perdition, a way that he shall know. Thereupon the tender Prince informs the prostrate and sinful minstrel that a band of pilgrims are now assembled from every part of Thuringia, who are resolved to seek the sacred shrine at Rome, and he advises Tannhäuser to accompany them and seek pardon of the Holy Father, nor return again until such grace is given. Elizabeth adds her soft beseechments to the Landgrave's counsel, an influence which Tannhäuser cannot resist, and begging forgiveness of the maid whom he has basely betrayed, as a chorus of young Pilgrims is heard in the distance he staggers from the hall crying "To Rome! To Rome!"

Act III.—The setting of Scene I. in the third act is the same as in Act I., showing the valley below the Wartburg. The time is near sunset, and Elizabeth is seen kneeling before a shrine, deeply engaged in prayer. Wolfram is descending a mountain path, and as he draws near he discovers the love-lorn maid, which prompts him to soliloquize, "By yonder shrine I'm ever sure to find her," etc., praying that heaven may shrive the sinner. Wolfram has long loved Elizabeth, but so pure, unselfish and withal so magnanimous are his feelings that he will not seek his own advancement at the expense of the maid's true happiness, nor wish evil of his rival, whose soul is crying from out the deeps. Rather does he pray that Tannhäuser may return, absolved, to bless the maid.

"Ye saints, oh, grant their happy meeting;
Although my wound may never heal,
Oh, may she ne'er my anguish feel!"

At this moment the chant of Pilgrims is heard, at which Elizabeth arises, exclaiming: "They have returned! Ye saints, oh, let me know my task, that I may worthily fulfill it."

The procession draws near, and as they pass, one by one, the poor maid eagerly scans each face till the last are gone, when finding that Tannhäuser is not among them, she falls upon her knees and pours out her soul of anguish to the Blessed Virgin.

"Here in the dust I bend before thee.
Now from this earth, oh set me free," etc.

"O thou sublime, sweet evening star,"

As Elizabeth rises from her supplications, Wolfram advances and asks permission to guide her to the castle, but she answers by no word, and bids him by gesture not to speak to her; then turning her face she moves up the mountain path, eagerly, though painfully, watched by Wolfram until she passes beyond his sight. Then as the creeping shades of evening envelop the forest, and the stars begin to appear one by one, "Like death's dark shadow, night her gloom extendeth," he sings:

"O thou sublime, sweet evening star.
Joyful I greet thee from afar;
Oh greet for me as passing by,
From earth's green valleys to the sky;
One to whom all my heart was given,
An angel soon to be in heaven," etc.

This song is the serenest gem of the opera, and composes an effective prelude to what immediately follows, for as the last strains expire, a lone figure, grimed with the dust of the highway, bent under the burdens of exposure, worn by disappointment, and struggling with hopeless guilt, appears before Wolfram, who asks,

"Who art thou, Pilgrim,
Thy lonely path pursuing?"

Wolfram fails to detect at first view the outcast minstrel, under so sorry an exterior, but Tannhäuser knows his friend, the wise and generous Wolfram, and calling his name, the recognition is complete. Amazed more by his friend's appearance than by his return, Wolfram eagerly inquires: "What means thy coming thus dejected?"

Tannhäuser, broken in spirit, guilt oppressed, answers with profound humility, betraying his sense of hopelessness, "Have no fear, I seek thee not nor yet thy companions, but a path that leads to Venus' hill!"

Wolfram is shocked by the unholy ambition of his friend, who has manifestly returned as a voluptuary from his pilgrimage of penance, with soul steeped in sin. Grieved and angered by Tannhäuser's frailty, Wolfram conjures him to tell if he has been to Rome, promising to hear with compassion if he has sued for pardon. By such exhortation Tannhäuser is persuaded to relate what has befallen him; to tell the pitiable story of his sufferings; to confess how his petition for grace and absolution has been denied.

The jaded traveler speaks of how, contrite in spirit, he bent his steps to Rome to reconcile offended heaven; of how unshod he walked amid the rocks and thorns, bared his head forlorn to the brazen sun, nor refreshed his lips at cooling fountain; with wasted heart, for the sake of an angel, Rome was gained at last, where with tears imploring he knelt before the rood in faith adoring, before him who holds the keys of heaven. And thousands the Pope forgave and blessed that day, but when he, the suppliant, made his plaint, and in despair confessed the mad desires that had darkened his soul, the sinful pleasures by which he was long enslaved, craving in dust and tears a gracious word, the Holy Father answering spake:

> "If thou hast shared the joys of hell;
> If thou unholy flames has nursed
> That in the hill of Venus dwell,
> Thou art forever more accursed;
> And as this barren ——
> Ne'er will put forth ——
> Thus shalt thou ——
> Salvation or ——"

Thus spurned by the holy presence the penitent, in dumb hopelessness first bereft of sense ... until the evening songs of praise and prayer disturbed the air with joyful sound. Outcast with horror in his breast, he turned and fled from Rome ... retrieved, sin-cursed, beyond expiation, Tannhäuser cries out:

> "Thus I spend my sinful hours, joys to taste again,
> Which once before my earthborn flame had slain;
> To thee, fair Venus, I surrender ——
> ——
> I'll be thy slave, love-slav'd of ——"

Wolfram in vain tries to stay his godless ravings, but Tannhäuser cannot be opposed. Cursed by God and spurned by men, he will seek surcease in the arms of Venus, whom he beseeches to guide him to her retreat of sensual pleasure. Nor does he call in vain, for Venus appears, in radiant form, attended by flying nymphs to receive her recreant slave, and answers

> "I welcome thee, perfidious man;
> Earth laid thee low beneath its ban;
> Hast thou by all then been forsaken;
> In my arms blissfully to awaken?"

Wolfram endeavors to dispel the hellish phantoms, entreating his friend to repent and find salvation; but the dancing sirens, in swirl of abandon, and the call of Venus, "Oh, come, beloved, forever thou art mine," more madly steeps his soul with guilty desire, and with impatience he refuses longer to listen to the implorations of him who points the way to redemption. With hope of winning him from the embraces of the goddess Wolfram cries after him, "Do you not hear an angel's supplication, who now for thee his grace implores—*Elizabeth?*"

As this sainted name is spoken, Tannhäuser exclaims in anguish, "Oh, maid divine!" at which Venus and her train of sporting nymphs are dispersed, uttering shrieks of rage as they disappear. The morning now breaks and a funeral hymn is borne upon the air. As Tannhäuser turns his gaze from the flight of the sensual throng he perceives a procession approaching, carrying upon an open bier the body of a beautiful maiden. As the bearers draw near Tannhäuser recognizes that it is Elizabeth, the sweet saint who has died of love, using her last breath in prayer for his salvation. The sight overwhelms him in an ocean of remorse, and crying, "Holy Saint Elizabeth, oh, pray for me," he expires beside the bier.

At this moment a body of pilgrims appear bearing the Pope's staff which suddenly puts forth leaves and blossoms, as a symbol that the repentant sinner is redeemed.

> "The Lord himself now thy bondage hath riven,—
> Go enter with the blest in heaven."

AMBROISE THOMAS.

EW composers have achieved such lasting fame by a single composition as did the subject of this sketch. His bright particular creation shines with such superior lustre as to obscure nearly all his lesser productions, which though numerous none other have so charmed the popular ear, or added much to his reputation. "Mignon" (produced in 1860), though it may not be admitted to the list of great operas, has the flattering distinction of being one of the most highly favored and generally admired in the modern repertory, a chief position from which it may not soon be dislodged. The plot is one of remarkable interest, but is really secondary to the music, which throughout is vivid, picturesque and intensely delightful. "Hast Thou E'er Seen the Land," the duet between Mignon and the old harpist; the pretty gavot, tenor solo, " Adieu, Mignon," and the brilliant overture, are imperishable things in the world of song.

Charles Louis Ambroise Thomas was a native of Lorraine, born in Metz, August 5, 1811. His parents were well to do, and gave Charles the benefits of a finished education, designing that he should adopt a profession, preferably that of the law, but this purpose was promptly changed by the youth's fondness for music and his urgent desire to be permitted to pursue that study. At the close of his seventh year at school, and when fourteen years of age, he was sent to the Paris Conservatory, where it was his good fortune to become a pupil of such famous instructors as Zimmerman, Kalkbrenner, Dourlen, Barbereau and Le Sueur, under whom he studied successively the piano-forte, harmony, counterpoint and composition, exhibiting much proficiency in each branch. In 1829, when only eighteen years of age, he won the first prize for piano-forte, his playing, as was declared at the time, exhibiting extraordinary skill. The year following he was awarded the prize for harmony, and in 1832 he submitted as his graduation composition, a dramatic cantata entitled "Herman et Ketty," which gained for him the Grand Prix de Rome, the highest honor that is bestowed upon graduating pupils of the Conservatory. Having secured this scholarship, which entitled him to a finishing course at the expense of the French Government, he proceeded at once to Rome, where he continued his studies for a period of three years, after which he traveled a year and visited all the European capitals.

In 1836 Ambroise, as he was always familiarly called, returned to Paris to devote himself to lyrical composition, which he pursued industriously but without distinguished results until his production of "Mignon," which was received on its first presentation with great acclamation, and gave him immediate fame. Though this favor of fortune was not obtained until 1866, he had given many proofs of genius by minor creations, which was duly recognized by several elections. Thus, in 1845, he was made a member of the Legion of Honor; in 1851 he became a member of the Academy; in 1856 an officer, and in 1858 a commander; but singular to relate is the fact that though "Mignon," his masterpiece, was received with the greatest favor not only in France, but in all the musical centres of Europe, it brought him no other honor than that of public appreciation and generous recompense. In 1871, however, his largest ambition was realized, when by the death of Auber (May 12), the position of director of the Paris Conservatory became vacant, to which Thomas was promptly elected.

Under the able directorship of Auber the Conservatory, always affectionately and pridefully regarded, gained a loftier reputation, which was further increased by the wise administration of Thomas, who devoted his energies and all his mental resources to promoting its interests. For a period of twenty-five years did this popular composer foster, with delicate care and generous encouragement, the musical tastes and talents not alone of his countrymen, but of aspirants of other nationalities, until the Conservatory became the first institution of its kind in Europe, which reputation is maintained by the equally able directorship of his successor, M. Theodore Dubois. Thomas produced altogether seventeen operas, his latest works being "Francois de Rimini" in 1882, and "La Tempete," a ballet, in 1889, neither of which has survived. He died in Paris, February 12, 1896.

AMBROISE THOMAS

1

Mignon

(AFTER THE ORIGINAL PAINTING BY WILLIAM DE LEFTWICH DODGE)

LOTARIO—"*Mignon, Gugliehno, I do greet ye!*
Welcome, to this my house!"

ACT III   SCENE VIII.

MIGNON.

Music by Ambroise Thomas.—Libretto by Carré and Barbier.

GERMAN literature, rich and splendid as it is, would be as impoverished by the exclusion of Goethe's works as would be our own by removal of those of Shakespeare, and the world would be sadly bereft should the productions of either be destroyed. Goethe has created so much and always with wonderful manifestation of the highest genius, that since his death admirers among many nations have been trying in vain to determine which one of his works,—poems, legends, stories, dramas,— is entitled to the rank of supreme excellence. Possibly a majority of cultured persons familiar with his writings will give the palm to "Wilhelm Meister," the plot of which story is sympathetically charming and the style soft and flowing. It has about it all the sweetness and simplicity that distinguishes his melancholic but seductive "Werther," and possesses the added interest of mellowness and maturity, being written at a time when his faculties were strongest and his capacity greatest.

It was the very sad but tenderly lovable story of "Wilhelm Meister" that Ambroise Thomas chose for lyrical dramatization under the title of "Mignon," who is the principal character in Goethe's novel. The adaptation preserves the general story of the author, but considerable license was taken by the collaborators, who introduced not a few changes, such as seemed necessary to them to adapt it perfectly to operatic purposes. Several of the most dramatic features and the identical language are retained, however, among which is especially to be noted Mignon's song, "Hast Thou E'er Seen the Land."

The first production of "Mignon" was at the Opera Comique, Paris, November 17, 1866, upon which memorable occasion the cast of leading characters was as follows: Mignon, Mme. Galli-Marie; Wilhelm Meister, M. Achard; Laertes, M. Conders; Lotario, M. Bataille; Filina, Mme. Cabal. The opera was received with very great favor at its first presentation, and grew in popularity so rapidly that within a year following it had been translated and given before intensely delighted audiences in nearly all the capitals of Europe. To-day "Mignon" is sung with much frequency in the cities of every civilized country, and its reputation is secure as it is great.

Act I, Scene I.—The curtain rises upon a scene that represents the court-yard of a German Inn before which are the customary drink tables, where both town and country people are being served with beer. While drinking, the men sing in chorus of the festive day, of mirth and joy, the happy time of great and small, when with cigars and beer the hours are beguiled. While the company is thus singing, Lotario, an aged harper, appears at the tavern entrance, and advancing slowly to the middle of the court-yard sings a plaintive song, with harp accompaniment, whereby he tells of his long and wretched wanderings searching for his only child, Mignon, who many years ago was stolen from him by strolling gypsies.

The Inspiration of Wilhelm Meister

Lotario's bent form, his looks of sorrow, and his song of woe, excite the compassion of many of the drinkers, who invite him to take a seat, and filling a glass for him they repeat the verse which they were singing when he entered.

Scene II.—A band of gypsies of both sexes now appear, who stop to give an entertainment to the people. The gypsies march round the stage preceded by a cart loaded with old camp utensils, and with Mignon, who, wrapped in a tattered mantle, is sleeping on a sheaf of straw. Zaffi, one of the performers, gives the signal for a dance by starting a lively tune upon his violin, seconded by oboe and tambourine. Filina and Laertes watch the performance with much interest from an overlooking balcony, giving approving words and complimenting the happy disposition and dexterity of the gypsies. Giarno, chief of the band, finding the audience thoroughly appreciative, who by liberal gift of coins attest their pleasure, tells them that to show his sense of obligation he will now have Mignon give them a sample of her skill by performing the far-famed "egg dance." Thereupon, turning to Zaffi he tells him to prepare to sing his

MIGNON

choicest song and instructs others to spread upon the ground their beauteous piece of carpet, which being carefully disposed, a boy advances and places several eggs upon it, leaving but little space between for the dancer's flying feet.

Ciarno goes to the cart and arouses Mignon, who is made to appear bearing in her hand a bouquet of wild flowers, but her face is hidden by a mantle. Filina cries to Ciarno:

> "What, ho! good sir, permit me to inquire
> What hapless being is that just waking?
> Say, is't a girl, or stripling lad?"

Ciarno answers her that it is neither woman, girl nor boy, at which Filina laughs heartily, asking, "What is it then, I pray?" Ciarno removes the mantle and replies, "'Tis Mignon!" At sight of the unveiled girl the company laugh, which causes her great confusion, thinking that the rude company mean to mock and insult her. As she stands irresponsive to the music, Ciarno coarsely commands her to dance, but she stamps her foot and stubbornly refuses. Ciarno's expression at once becomes lowering, and in great anger he takes a stick from one of his companions and again commands her to dance. She still refuses, and he lifts the cudgel to strike, but Lotario encircles Mignon in his arms, begging her to take heart, that he her shield will be, if she will fly hence. Ciarno pushes poor old Lotario violently and again orders Mignon to dance or bear swift punishment for her disobedience. At the moment Ciarno is about to strike, Guglielmo (Wilhelm Meister), a young student on his travels, enters, followed by his servant carrying a portmanteau.

Scene III.—Quick to notice the threatening purpose of the brutal gypsy chief, Guglielmo grasps his uplifted arm and fiercely cries, "Ruffian, hold, or meet thy death!" Ciarno is disposed to savagely resent the student's interference, but seeing a pistol enforcing Guglielmo's demands, he piteously exclaims, "I am ruined; who will repay me for the loss I thus endure?" Filina, with divided sympathy, throws a purse to the gypsy, but bids him hold his tongue, and take his leave quickly. Mignon, grateful for her deliverance, divides her bouquet, giving half to Guglielmo and half to Lotario, as tokens of her thankfulness. Filina, fascinating of manner, is an adept in the practice of such artful ways as beguile susceptible youths, and these she uses with such effect upon Guglielmo that he directly conceives a violent passion for the actress to whom, in a concerted piece, he sings:

MIGNON, THE GYPSIES' SLAVE.

> "So strange an occurrence
> Who e'er could foresee?
> Nature's own instincts
> My steps did hither bend."

Filina has not looked upon the chivalrous young student with disinterested eyes, but with such concern that she eagerly asks Laertes to tell her who the gentleman can be whose manners are so urbane, which Laertes is not able to fully answer, but he perceives how deeply Filina is charmed, and therefore replies with bantering speech. Mignon has drawn apart and bowing prays to the Holy Virgin, while Lotario in fixed abstraction sweeps aimlessly the strings of his harp for a while, then sings:

> "The shades of evening began to fall,
> When through the forest dark and drear,
> A knight all clad in steel of proof
> Did slowly wend his way."

All the townsfolk and gypsies now withdraw, and Ciarno retires, followed by Mignon and Lotario. Filina disappears from the balcony into her room, as Laertes descends a stairway to speak with Guglielmo, whom he has signaled.

Scene IV.—Laertes salutes Guglielmo and praises him for rendering such knightly succor to a helpless maid, and tells him that Filina is no less pleased with his gallant conduct. Filina, Laertes explains,

"'Tis time I should speak but I am weary of doing thy bidding."

is, like himself, the remnant of a luckless troupe of actors, who hopes for a prosperous turn of fortune's wheel, but for himself he curses in his heart the Tragic Muse. Guglielmo seeks to console the impoverished player by ordering two flagons of wine, over which they talk of Filina, with expressions of mutual admiration, Laertes at length declaring:

> "She's flighty, vain, cantankerous, astute,
> Fickle as fortune, and more changeable
> Than is the moon!
> And yet her beauty rare,
> With love all hearts inflame –
> Let's drink her health!"

Scene V.—Filina has overheard the conversation, and cautiously descending she comes upon Laertes suddenly and touching him on the shoulder with her fan, haughtily speaks, "So, sir! since you have finished the picture why not place it in a frame?" Guglielmo courteously interposes, "Those bright eyes such calumny soon dispel!"

She expresses her gratitude for this gracefully turned compliment and then, aside, speaks her resolve to exercise her charms to win his love, pridefully believing that no youthful heart can resist her. Turning then to Guglielmo, she makes sport of Laertes, who has not the grace to win a fair lady and hence affects to despise them. Laertes, feeling the sting of Filina's irony, obtains a measure of satisfaction by introducing the two, taking advantage to declare that Filina, an actress of merit and renown, has been much taken with the student and desires greatly to let him know it. Aside to Guglielmo, he tells him to present his nosegay to the gentle lady, but taking it from Guglielmo's hand, he gives it to Filina himself, thus causing them both much embarrassment. After some artless speech and many exchanges of compliments Filina takes Laertes' arm and the two depart, leaving Guglielmo alone.

Scene VI.—Mignon appears, coming from a shed, and coyly approaching Guglielmo says her master sleeps and she craves the privilege of kissing his hand. The student with little sympathy tells her that on the morrow he will be so far from her that further aid he can never give. "To-morrow!" she feverishly replies, "Why, it is known alone to God where we shall be to-morrow." Touched now by her gratitude and pitiful speech, Guglielmo asks Mignon about her parents. "My mother died long ago," she answers, "and my first master dying I was sold to another whom you have just seen." Urged to tell her remembrance Mignon relates:

> "Alas! of my entire infancy one souvenir alone is left me.
> 'Twas dusk! Along a broad lane's bank I ran,
> When suddenly, a crowd of men
> Whose faces were to me unknown, did press around me
> A piercing shriek I uttered and through the fields
> I headlong hurried, but was caught and taken."

Thrilled by her broken story, Guglielmo begs her to tell him of her childhood recollections, and encourages her by asking if he should set her free, what beloved spot would she seek? To this inquiry Mignon sings a beautifully pathetic solo:

> "Hast thou e'er seen the land
> Where the wild citron grows." etc.

Guglielmo tells the homeless girl that a spot so enchanted must surely be Italy, but she answers, "Alas! I cannot say," so long has been her captivity among the strolling gypsies.

Scene VII.—At this moment Giarno comes running upon the scene and sarcastically addresses Guglielmo: "Oho, the damsel pleases you, it seems!"

With a firm hand Guglielmo seizes the gypsy by the coat and fiercely commands him to utter not another word. Trembling with fear, Giarno promises silence, but tells the student that since he is so pleased with Mignon he will sell her for a price, which proposal Guglielmo joyously accepts and the two retire within the tavern to consummate the bargain.

Scene VIII.—As the two disappear Mignon, unable to restrain her joy, shouts in ecstasy of feeling, Free! Free! And is it really true?" Lotario now emerges from the shed, at sight of whom Mignon rapturously begs him to share her joy, and to accept her gratitude for having defended her. Lotario replies that he has come to take his leave; that as the swallows southward fly, so must he follow. She eagerly asks why she may not go with him, and taking the minstrel's harp she strikes the strings and sings:

"Oh, swallows gay and blithe."

This song is interrupted by the loud laughter of Filina, and Mignon and Lotario withdraw to the inn as Filina, Federico and Guglielmo appear.

Scene IX.—Filina laughs mockingly at Federico, who dusting his clothes, reproves himself for having exhausted his horse racing after her. And while the two are exchanging reproaches, Giarno appears at the door of the inn, to whom Guglielmo speaks, "'Tis understood then—Mignon is free!"

Scene X.—Filina, addressing Guglielmo, asks, "Hear I aright? Has Mignon been purchased from her master?" which he has no need to answer, for Giarno returns to the shed, felicitating himself upon so good a bargain. Seeing Filina talking with Guglielmo, Federico, who is deeply in love with the actress, jealously interposes, whereat Filina introduces him:

— Signor Guglielmo,
Permit me to introduce my young friend Federico.
Who whether I will or no
My cavalier doth undertake to be:
A rack brained but good humored youth.
Sadly addicted to boiling over
With mad fits of furious jealousy!"

And the two continue their badinage until Laertes calls Filina.

Scene XI.—As Laertes enters he greets Federico heartily, but the latter's good humor is quickly dissipated by Filina, who mocks him with jeers and laughter, flouting his claim of having ridden a good horse to death all on her account. At which Laertes interposes to add ridicule to Federico's hurts by remarking, "Alas! the ill-starred animal—Of course I mean the horse!" Federico being angered by such banter, turns away, and Laertes addresses Filina, telling her that their adverse fortunes at length have changed and admonishes her to be quick in getting ready to perform her part; then producing a letter addressed to her he bids her read it, but she affecting diffidence, requests that he perform this service, whereupon he breaks the seal and reads:

— Beauteous Goddess!
Wishing right worthily to celebrate
The Prince Ubirio Tieffenbach's arrival,
I hope to see you, with your friends,
(At whose head I trust Laertes to behold !)
At this my castle, ere day declines.
I trust the invitation will be pleasing to you.
You well know the flame
Which burns within my tender heart.
A carriage now awaits you—should you refuse.
You will be carried here by force.
— Baron Rosenberg."

MIGNON.

Federico is astounded when he hears the letter read, for the baron is his uncle, and such a declaration of passionate admiration gives him to understand that he has a new and most embarrassing rival. But his discomfiture is soon to be greatly increased. Filina is transported by the prospect of retrieving her fortune, and availing herself of the baron's permission to invite any guests she may choose, she asks Guglielmo to accompany her. Federico has anticipated this pleasure, and when cruelly told that he may find the way himself if he would persist in following her, he becomes frantic with humiliation and despair. As Filina now leaves to prepare for her journey, Laertes admonishes Guglielmo to listen no longer to the cajoleries and deceits of the coquette, who has no other aim than to make her admirers miserable, as she has made Federico. But though hesitating for a time, Guglielmo rejects the counsel of Laertes, who enters the Inn, and decides to follow her.

Scene XII.—Mignon now appears and asks Guglielmo, since she belongs to him by right of purchase, to make such disposition of her as may please his will. Ignorant of the passion that Mignon feels for him, and charmed by Filina, Guglielmo is embarrassed by the presence of the girl, and proposes that she accept a home with an aged relative who lives within the town. With sorrowful expression, she appeals, "Must I then part from thee?"

"Why, my child, I cannot be always with you to act the part of father!" is the comfortless reply he gives her.

Mignon, guided by love, as well as by gratitude, suggests that she disguise herself as a servant and travel with him, which service she will regard joyfully, as thereby her thankfulness may be shown. Guglielmo expresses surprise that, ransomed from one master, she esteems her liberty so lightly as to willingly become immediately slave to another, whereat Mignon is so grieved that she turns to Lotario, who at the moment appears, and offers to depart with him. The old minstrel's heart leaps with joy at this proposal, and he attempts to draw her with him, but Guglielmo, betraying anxiety for her future with a wandering minstrel, interposes, and shows his resolve to accept his new responsibility by telling her to adopt the disguise of a page, and attend him on his travels. Mignon is transported by this decision of her student master, and so kisses his hand with rapture that Guglielmo's heart is touched with pity, from which a spark of love is kindled that presently flames into strongest passion.

Scene XIII.—A noise is heard outside the inn and immediately after a crowd of townspeople, gypsies, and country folk appear to announce the coming of a troupe of actors, who follow quickly after. Among the latter are Laertes, Filina, and Ciarno, all on the way to Baron Rosenberg's castle, who sing in chorus of their new fortune in being invited to entertain so rich a host. Everything being in readiness for their departure Filina bids Guglielmo join them, urging her invitation in a beautiful song. "You'll come with us, I trust, sir." Guglielmo hesitates between love and duty, but presently excuses himself with a promise to follow as soon as possible. Hoping to overcome his decision, Filina shows him the flowers which a short while before he gave her, as if to ask, "Does your admiration fade so soon as these?" At this moment Mignon comes from the little shed and seeing in Filina's hand the nosegay which she gave to Guglielmo as a token

"*** ****, *****, *** **** *****."

of her gratitude, mournfully reproaches him by calling his attention to how carefully Lotario has preserved the flowers she gave him, so unlike his own disregard for her gift of gratitude. Brought to confusion by Mignon's words, that evidences how deeply she has been wounded, Guglielmo dissembles, by speaking in an aside, "I did not give it, child,—'twas stolen from me." But Mignon is not entirely reassured, and anxious to bring about a separation between Filina and Guglielmo she urges the gypsies to depart, first distributing some little gifts among them, and attaching a medal about the neck of a lad of the tribe as a talisman for his safety. Farewells are now spoken, hurried preparations are made, and with

MIGNON

feelings of hilarity over pleasurable anticipations of the approaching entertainment, the happy group set out upon their journey for Baron Rosenberg's castle. This scene affords a climax for the first act, upon which the curtain falls.

Act II. Scene 1.—The opening scene of Act II discloses Filina in her boudoir, dressing herself to represent "Titania" for the forthcoming performance of "Midsummer Night's Dream" at the baron's castle. While thus engaged she passes vain compliments upon herself, and sings of the many conquests which she has made. While Filina is seated before the glass, with her back towards the door, Laertes enters, who, overhearing her self-congratulations, sings in derision of her boastings, quite as much expressive of his own present good fortune:

"A pasion of kisses I already see before me."

"Naught to me such joy affords
As wine which I drink without cost," etc.

Then addressing Filina, he excuses his presence by telling her he has come to see if her preparations are complete, but before he is able to speak as seriously as he has intended, he observes Guglielmo, who enters rather diffidently, leaving Mignon on the outside. Laertes, though very much in love with Filina, is afraid to declare himself, lest his present pleasure of association and hope be destroyed by a decisive refusal; but to commend himself in her eyes as a magnanimous person he gracefully speaks to Guglielmo of Filina's beauty as a woman, and of her talents as an actress, and then with profound deference to both he turns to retire. As he is about to go out he draws back in surprise at seeing Mignon, who, dressed as a page, has been standing by the door, waiting the demands of her new master. At Guglielmo's suggestion, Mignon is invited to enter, but she is greeted with ill-concealed jealousy by Filina, who sneeringly tells her she may come and warm herself, for perhaps she will then condescend to amuse them with the "egg dance." Laertes is quick to observe the gathering clouds of rage upon Filina's brow and to escape the threatening storm of jealousy he dissembles by a show of illness and discreetly takes his leave.

Scene III.—Guglielmo betrays much anxious solicitude for the comfort of Mignon, seating her in an arm chair and tenderly adjusting her position to receive the genial warmth, which draws from Mignon such expressions of loving gratitude that Filina is provoked to sneeringly observe:

"What touching anxiety!
Excuse me if I laugh
At this reciprocal solicitude!"

and again, laughing, she declares she is moved by such tender attentions, for:

"Instead of waiting on his master,
It is the master who doth wait upon his page."

Guglielmo, touched with pride, and really charmed by Filina, is unable longer to resist her fascinations, and offers to do her homage far more zealous if she will accept his proffered service. Whereupon, to test his devotion, she seats herself again by her toilet table and commands him to hold for her the candelabra, by which light she will rearrange her hair in a manner which she hopes will please him. The two now render a gay duet, "Charming Gay Compliments," in which the most affectionate sentiments are expressed and Guglielmo develops the enthusiasm of an ardent lover who is unable to restrain the extravagance of his passion. Filina, while secretly rejoicing over her conquest, feigns anxiety to proceed to the baron's presence, there to introduce him, but Guglielmo stops her to ask, "Will you not answer me?" For reply she extends her hand, which he fervidly kisses, and promises to be—merciful. Mignon, with her head inclined upon her chair, has simulated sleep during this passage of declaration, but she startles at the sound of Guglielmo's kiss upon Filina's hand, though she is too discreet to discover to them what she has heard. Guglielmo continues his vows and impassioned utterances, which Filina listens to with such poor patience that she would suspend his praise in order to tell him how others have been worshipers of her rare beauty. While thus

"From death I have saved her."

flattering, Guglielmo offers Filina his arm and the two walk off together, leaving Mignon alone in the room to console her jealous wrath, to nurse her heart wounds, and to reflect upon the misery which unrequited love entails.

Scene IV.—When Mignon discovers that she is alone, in a sumptuously furnished room, she at first bewails her luckless love, but soon banishes misery by absorption in examining and contemplating the rich adornments of Filina's chamber. Perceiving a rouge-pot she quickly paints her cheeks and looking in the glass she sings a coquettish song, called a "Styrienne," which though "a mad story," is the most popular number of the opera. Infatuated with her improved appearance the thought seizes her to add to her charms the embellishments of fine dress, to obtain which she goes into a cabinet where Filina's wardrobe is kept.

Scene V.—In the temporary absence of Mignon, Federico enters the room, unattended, and looking about, to find that he is alone, he sings an exquisite rondo gavotte, expressive of his determination to win Filina, to compel her love, and claim the victory, even though she be a cruel flirt.

Scene VI.—Guglielmo now returns from a walk with Filina, and from a rear door calls Mignon, but getting no answer he enters, to be confronted by Federico. The two, after passing some courtesies, fall to questioning each other as to their respective purposes in visiting Filina's room, until Federico, much angered, draws his sword and bids Guglielmo defend himself. The young student hesitates to wage a combat in Filina's room, but is so provokingly challenged that he finally consents to dispute the rivalry by trial at arms, placing himself in an attitude of defiance.

Scene VII.—As Guglielmo and Federico are upon the point of falling upon each other with drawn swords, Mignon rushes out of the cabinet arrayed in Filina's finery, and throwing herself between the jealous combatants commands them to suspend their violence.

Both men are confounded with surprise by the suddenness of this splendid apparition, scarcely trusting their senses to believe that it is the little gypsy girl, the demure and forlorn Mignon, who stands before them. Federico's anger gives way to mirth when he observes that Mignon is appareled in borrowed plumage, and with hearty laugh he leaves the room.

Scene VIII.—Guglielmo, giving voice to his astonishment, seriously asks Mignon if she has lost her reason, or what has prompted to such strange caprice? Mignon begs to be forgiven for her folly, but Guglielmo is unwilling to excuse her audacity, and in an aria tells her they must part. As she utters a cry of grief and throws herself into a chair, he bids her take courage and not weep:

"O'er thee, just heaven will watch with fostering care,
Oh mayst thou thy dear native land once more regain!"

Mignon, most sorrowfully, bestows her thanks, but asks that since they must part she may be allowed to wander freely. At which Guglielmo begs to know what she will do when he withdraws his care. "That which I did before," she answers. "I will Mignon once more become; the gypsy rags I hasten now to don." Guglielmo, with compassion for her grief, offers her a purse, which she refuses, asking no other favor than permission to kiss his hand, while he in tones of anguish exclaims, "Oh, grievous trial!"

Scene IX.—Filina enters and interrupts the painful scene. With exclamation of astonishment she discovers Mignon to be wearing her clothes, but Guglielmo, with manifest confusion, pleads that she be excused, as her prompting is only a whim. Filina, however, continues to sarcastically remark upon the change of the gypsy girl, and to look so disdainfully upon her that Mignon is unable to endure the scornful reproaches longer, and tearing Filina's livery from her person she runs from the hateful presence of her imperious rival. Filina expresses to Guglielmo her belief that Mignon is in the throes of a jealous rage, at which he asks, "Why jealous?" not as yet appreciating that Mignon's feelings for him are ardent love more than profound gratitude. Laertes, dressed for the play, appears to admonish Filina that the performance is about to begin, at which she tells Guglielmo if he truly loves her to accept her arm, and thus together the two pass out. Federico suddenly issues from an apartment on the left in time to see the couple leaving, at which sight his jealousy is ungovernable, and he hurls an imprecation at Guglielmo, while Mignon having resumed her gypsy garb, reappears a moment, to exclaim, "That woman! I loathe her!"

A series of tableaux follow, the first of which represents a park adjoining the baron's castle, in which are to be seen a conservatory illuminated, and a lake with reeds fringing the margin. Mignon enters alone and sings of her wretchedness, of her aching heart breaking from unrequited love, until seeing the lake she rashly resolves to ease her misery by seeking surcease beneath the waves. When about to cast herself into the water her ears catch the music of a harp from behind the trees, and turning about she recognizes Lotario, whereupon her evil resolution is at once abandoned, and she expresses a wish to live, whatever fate may prove.

Scene II.—Lotario does not at first perceive that it is Mignon who addresses him, but when called to mind he tenderly embraces and begs her tell him all her griefs. Appreciative of this healing sympathy, Mignon, with plaintive speech, asks if he has ever languished, hopeless, in despair, vainly seeking his native land, for such alone will enable him to understand the sorrow which she now endures.

"Ang sta of the worthy mansion, I was once the lord."

Answering, the old minstrel assures her that such cruel suffering has been his lot, wandering through foreign lands in quest of one whom he cannot find. At this moment a tumultuous noise of clapping hands is heard which Mignon understands is the applause that admiring friends are giving Filina, and in wrathful, jealous feelings she looks towards the conservatory while she imprecates:

"Oh, why does not avenging ire
Strike down and crush yon impious dwelling?"

and then as if shameful of her malediction she rushes away and disappears among the trees.

In Scene III Lotario, left alone, repeats to himself, "Fire, she said! Ah, fire! fire!" and slowly crossing the stage he enters the forest shades, as the door of the conservatory opens, and a crowd of guests and actors issue forth.

Scene IV—Gentlemen, ladies, Filina, actors, Federico, the baron, baroness, prince and servants with torches, come upon the stage, the performance being concluded, who, in chorus, praise the beauty and wondrous talent of Filina, whereupon she sings a beautiful recitative, "Yes, for this eve I shall reign queen of the fairies."

Scene V.—As the song concludes Guglielmo, Mignon and Lotario enter, the former of whom Filina chides gently for not being present at the performance, at which attention Federico is jealously irritated. Guglielmo, instead of responding, appears pre-occupied, and when pressed, admits that he is in search of Mignon. Filina forces her company upon him, however, and the two retire conversing. Lotario and Mignon meet and the minstrel, sotto voce, tells her that the wish which she has just expressed is to be fully gratified, for the conservatory has been fired by his own hands. Mignon looks horrified and stands in mute abstraction a moment until Guglielmo discovers her, when quickly leaving Filina he hurries to greet Mignon to express his joy at finding her. Filina, stung by jealous rage, intrudes upon the two and with a hope to rid herself of so dangerous a rival, and to subject her to humiliation, requests Mignon to enter the conservatory and there find and bring to her the bunch of "flowers which thou offeredst yesterday unto thy master, and which methinks have fallen from my bosom." Guglielmo would ask explanation of so strange a request, but Mignon hastens away to fulfill it. Scarcely has Mignon entered the conservatory when Filina makes discovery that the building is in flames, and gives the alarm. The servants hurry away with their torches, to render assistance, leaving the stage in utter darkness, which, however, is very soon lighted by the glare of conflagration. Guglielmo, realizing the danger which Mignon must endure, rushes through the crowd, repulsing all efforts to restrain him, and recklessly dashes into the blazing conservatory. All are in a state of great excitement, save alone Lotario, who moves about the stage singing a plaintive song of his quest for his child. With a loud crash the glasswork of the conservatory falls and the flames leap higher, out of the midst of which Guglielmo appears bearing the fainting Mignon in his arms, who, though unconscious, still grasps the withered flowers; which thrilling tableau concludes the second act.

Act III, Scene I.—When the curtain rises there is disclosed a gallery embellished with statues, and a harp prelude is heard behind the scenes, followed by a chorus. Lotario presently appears, and in Scene II he sings of sleeping Mignon. The action is now on the banks of one of the beautiful lakes of Italy, whither the suffering girl has been brought by Lotario and Guglielmo to recover her strength.

Scene III shows the interior of a fine mansion. Guglielmo and Antonio enter, the latter carrying a lamp which he sets upon a table, and then sings, in recitative, of to-morrow's festival on the lake shores, and of the mansion's desertion "since the thrice fatal day when woe so suddenly o'ertook its owners."

"I know it," answers Guglielmo; "I've been told that ten years ago a little girl was drowned in yonder waters."

Antonio sadly relates that the tragic accident killed the child's mother, and the father, crazed by grief, has gone hence, to wander, nor heard of more, the house being now for sale. Guglielmo, charmed by its sweet isolation, contemplates a purchase of the property and dismisses Antonio with a promise to speak with him on the morrow concerning the place.

Scene IV.—Guglielmo, turning to Lotario, asks what of Mignon; to which the old minstrel answers that she is peacefully sleeping, and her fever has abated. He then tells Lotario of his purpose to buy for Mignon's use the villa of Cipriani, which is the designation of the deserted mansion. At the pronouncement of this name Lotario starts violently, and after opening a long unused door he exclaims, "Ah, yonder!" exits slowly.

Scene V.—Guglielmo is alone, who, in soliloquy, tells how during her fever he has discovered that Mignon loves him, but vain have been his efforts to persuade confession of her feelings, and he sings, "Ah! little thought," etc.

Scene VI.—Lotario enters and gives Guglielmo a letter from Laertes, which, upon reading, he finds is a warning against the wiles and evil intents of Filina. With anxiety for Mignon, he starts towards her room, but perceiving that she is approaching stops beside the door.

Scene VII.—Mignon comes upon the stage so deeply absorbed with emotions aroused by her situation that she fails at first to discover her lover, and moving slowly forward a little way, in ecstatic abstraction she exclaims: "Where am I? What balmy air is this that now I breathe? Oh, how bright doth seem the blue of heaven!"

Gradually there dawns upon her a strange familiarity with the scene; indistinct remembrance of things she has seen before; dim recollections of place and surroundings "like to faint memories of one's childhood dreams." Bewildered and yet happy, she calls to Lotario and Guglielmo, who quickly responding, she throws herself into the latter's arms and in rapturous accents confesses her joy sublime. One of the sweetest duets ever heard upon the stage follows, which is interrupted by the voice of Filina, who is heard singing on the outside: "The Fair Titania am I: Titania, by all on earth beloved."

Surprised and shocked by the presence of the woman whom both have now cause to fear, Mignon sinks upon a seat wretched and comfortless, despite Guglielmo's assurances. Filina does not appear, and the encouragements of Guglielmo finally serve to restore Mignon to consciousness, who is persuaded to believe that the sound of Filina's voice was but a horrid dream. But she calls for Lotario, who soon appears upon the threshold, attired in a garb of black velvet, carrying a small treasure box in his hand.

Scene VIII.—Advancing, Lotario in confident voice bids the two welcome, saying: "Mignon, Guglielmo, I do gree ye! Welcome, to this my house."

MIGNON.

They cannot understand this strange language, nor the rich raiment with which the wandering aged minstrel is clothed, and they seeking explanation, Lotario tells them of his happy discovery; that his name is Cipriani, this house his own, from which long years before he strayed in quest of his child, who, though declared to have been drowned, he knew had been stolen. Then placing the coffer upon a table he invites Mignon to open it and possess herself of what is within. Quickly she responds, and lifting the contents finds a child's girdle, a beauteous thing that once belonged to Sperata. At this word Mignon startles: "Sperata! Sperata! The name doth seem familiar to my ear."

At this faint recognition by his child, Lotario gives way to tears, but absorbed in thoughts he asks if she does not also find a coral bracelet? Aye, it is here, but quite too small for such as she, whereupon Lotario lovingly tells her it was once too large, when she was child to wear it. Bidden to search further, Mignon produces a little prayer book, from which she begins reading aloud a prayer, the selfsame that Sperata repeated at close of day years agone. Overcome by a flood of memories thus started, Mignon falls in suppliant attitude and raising her eyes to heaven utters: "O Thou, who in heaven above all mortal hearts doth read," etc., being a continuation of the prayer learned at her mother's knee. Rising, with increased fervor she exclaims: "Lotario, mine! What secret proof's within my breast; I feel—I know—but yet cannot explain."

THE BALLET CONCLUSION OF MIGNON.

With violent effort she endeavors to recall her childhood recollections, then with a wild cry rushes through a door to reappear a moment later crying, "Yonder my mother's picture hangs!" At these words Lotario is assured that Mignon is Sperata, his long lost child, restored to him in God's providence to bless his life with priceless joy and compensate the woeful years of his wanderings.

Guglielmo rejoices in the happiness of their restoration, a bliss so great that Mignon faints from excitement. The solicitous lover hastens to her assistance crying: "Oh, dearest treasure, droop not thus!" Mignon presently revives, and unable longer to withhold confession of her love, she recompenses Guglielmo's devotion, and here in this enchanted spot the lovers abide, successors to the Casa Cipriani, the past forgotten, and the present a cup of joy filled for their draining.

BIOGRAPHICAL SKETCH OF GOUNOD.

CHARLES FRANCOIS GOUNOD was born in Paris, June 17, 1818. His father was an artist of much talent, but small means, and his mother was an ardent musician, so that the home influences were of the most refined and elevating character. The elder Gounod died when Charles was only five years of age, leaving so little property to his family that the widow maintained herself and two children by teaching music, in which school Charles quickly became the most promising pupil, and manifested such aptitude that after several years his mother's design to make him a notary was surrendered out of deference to both his wishes and his proficiency, and he was permitted to continue his musical studies. In 1836 Charles entered the Paris Conservatory, and at the same time took a course in the College of St. Louis, from which latter he graduated with the degree of LL. B., and in 1839 he was awarded the first prize for musical composition at the Conservatory, at which he submitted a cantata entitled "Fernand." Graduates of the Conservatory who achieve this honor are entitled to a course in the Italian school at the State's expense, so in 1840 Charles went to Rome, where for three years he applied himself with great perseverance to sacred music. Though for some time under the influence of Italian masters, Gounod had for his ideals Mozart and Meyerbeer, his personal sympathies inclining him especially toward the former, for whom his admiration was so great as to approach reverence.

CHARLES FRANCOIS GOUNOD.

Gounod returned to Paris in 1842, to accept the position of organist in the Missions Etrangeres, which he retained for several years, and became so devout that for a while he seriously contemplated renouncing the world to become a monastic. In 1843 he visited Vienna, where he was successful in procuring the performance of a mass in the Church of St. Paul, but returning to Paris, after a brief absence, he resumed his monastic garb and remained practically lost to sight until 1851, when he emerged from his retirement with his first opera, "Sappho," which was performed in that city, but met with so little favor that its repetition was not called for. In the following year he composed the choruses for Ponsard's classical tragedy, "Ulysses," which was sung in the Theatre Francais, to the unbounded praise and tumultuous applause of large and critical audiences. This so encouraged Gounod that he forgot the mental suffering which the failure of "Sappho" had caused him, and was inspired to attempt another lyrical composition, which he accomplished in 1854, in the production of "La Nonne Sanglante" ("The Bleeding Nun"), a grand opera in five acts. To his bitter disappointment, this was no more successful before the public than his first composition; but, undismayed, he applied his talent to the creation of a comic opera, entitled "Le Medecin Malgre Lui" ("The Mock Doctor"), which scored such a success as gave him a distinguished position among French composers of his time. Thus stimulated to greater effort by a generous reward, as well as appreciation, Gounod composed his immortal opera, "Faust," the initial performance of which, with Madame Carvalho, wife of the theatre manager, in the role of Marguerite, was given at the Theatre Lyrique, March 19, 1859, attended by the most enthusiastic demonstration, which served immediately to establish his fame for all time.

In 1860, Gounod's fourth opera, entitled "Philemon and Baucis," appeared. It was well received, and in 1862 was produced "La Reine de Saba" ("Queen of Sheba"), which likewise scored a fair success. One year later he composed a charming pastoral opera, entitled "Mireille," which achieved a popularity that time has scarcely lessened. Gounod was now so busy with performances of the operas which had won for him a great renown, that he ceased further composition for nearly three years, and it was not

BIOGRAPHICAL SKETCH OF GOUNOD

therefore until 1866 that his next opera appeared, entitled "La Colombe" ("The Pet Dove"), which, however, added nothing to his reputation. This was followed in 1867 by "Romeo and Juliet," a work of such decided merit that it may be placed next to his "Faust," and by not a few competent persons it is pronounced the equal of that beautiful composition. His later operatic productions were "Cinq Mars," 1877, "Polyeucte," an adaptation from Corneille's tragedy, 1878, and "Le Tribut de Zamora," 1880, none of which attained much popularity. His greatest sacred composition was an oratorio entitled "The Redemption" which was received with extraordinary favor and occupied the largest share of public attention at the Birmingham Festival, in 1882. "Mors et Vita" ("Death and Life") was written as a sequel to "The Redemption," and has shared its popularity, while many critics declare that it possesses even greater melodies. "The Redemption" was dedicated to Her Majesty, the Queen, and "Mors et Vita" to His Holiness, Leo XIII, for both of whom Gounod had a sincere admiration, amounting to affection. Another sacred composition, produced in 1851, was an "Ave Maria," first rendered at St. Martin's, said by many competent musicians to be the purest gem of all his works.

Of Gounod's numerous songs, among the best known are, "There Is a Green Hill Far Away," "Ring Out, Wild Bells," "When the Children Pray," "The Peace of God," and "Evening Lullaby."

THE GOUNOD VILLA, ST. CLOUD.

Gounod may not be called the founder of French opera, but his musical personality has been of the first importance in the development of both music and opera in France, while his influence has been all-pervading, and his fame was as honestly won as it is secure. Nor was his country insensible to his merits, for in Paris his popularity was almost unbounded. Recognition of his talents was not confined to applause in the opera house, for in 1866 he was honored by election as member of the Institute of France, which is the highest distinction that can be conferred in the nation, while musical societies of nearly every country in Europe admitted him to honorary membership.

Gounod was an industrious as well as a talented composer, for, though he wrote only eleven operas, his compositions comprise a long list, and of such a varied character as prove his rare versatility and uncommon genius. Besides being author of many hymns and songs, of which "Nazareth" is universally popular, he wrote a great deal of church music, and not a little that is of pronounced excellence, notably his "Messe Solenelle," a Stabat Mater, the oratorio of "Tobie," a de Profundis, an Ave Verum, St. Cecilia Mass, and the psalm, "By the Waters of Babylon." His orchestral compositions include such universally admired pieces as "Saltarello," "Funeral March of a Marionette," and the "Meditation."

Gounod returned to Paris, after a three years' residence in London where he went in 1871, and having accumulated a considerable fortune through his compositions, in 1861 he built a beautiful residence in the Place Malesherbes, opposite the statue of Alexander Dumas, père, where he lived as a gentleman and musician, and where his widow, an excellent lady, who was the daughter of M. Zimmerman, also a musician, continues to reside. But he had a summer home at St. Cloud, an inherited property of his wife's, where he expired, October 18, 1893.

There is a strange coincidence between the death of Gounod and Mozart, which becomes especially striking when we consider the almost reverent admiration which the former entertained for the great German master. As all cultured persons know, Mozart expired while conducting a requiem which he composed to be sung for the repose of his own soul. Gounod likewise wrote his own funeral hymn, and on Sunday afternoon of October 15, 1893, he sent for the organist of the Church of St. Cloud, to call at his home to hear the hymn and to make a piano score of it. On this occasion Gounod played the requiem with nerve and extraordinary beauty, evidently deeply impressed by the solemnity and sacred reflections which the music inspired. In the evening, while placing the score in his secretaire, he was suddenly seized with a stroke of paralysis and fell upon the floor in a state of unconsciousness, from which he never rallied, and expired three days later. The news of his death spread with rapidity, and caused profound sorrow throughout the musical world. Queen Victoria sent the widow a telegram of sympathy, in which she expressed her sorrow for the great loss that France and all Europe had sustained by reason of his death; while the municipality of Paris paid a splendid tribute to his fame by according to the remains one of the most magnificent funerals that ever attested the affections of the people of that city for one of its heroes.

Faust

MARGUERITE — "*A Goal! What voice thus calls in the darkness?*
What thick shadows descend on my soul!"

ACT IV — SCENE V

FAUST.

Music by Charles François Gounod.——Words by Barrier and Carre.

GOETHE'S famous tragedy affords the foundation for the Opera of Faust, which follows very closely those portions of the poem having reference particularly to the fortunes of Marguerite of Rouet. It was first produced at the Theatre Lyrique, Paris, March 19, 1859, and has ever since held its place in public estimation as one among the most popular of Grand Operas. The motive of the piece is to show the allurements of unlawful pleasures, the evil results attending their indulgence, and the certain retribution which is sure to follow the commission of sin, which is little mitigated by the common excuse of great temptation.

The opera is complete in five acts. The first scene opens in the early morning, revealing the learned alchemist, Dr. Faust, alone in his study. His life has been spent in an eager search after knowledge, science, magic, transmutation, but to the exclusion of all the gentle and refining influences of life, until in his old age he finds himself without friends or sympathetic surroundings. He has, in fact, reached that point at which all must arrive who attempt to solve the mysteries of nature without complying with the beneficent laws which she has thrown around us, and realizing too late, the emptiness of his life, the results of vain ambitions and selfishness, in the bitterness of his disappointment he exclaims

"Naught do I see! Naught do I know! Naught! Naught!"

There is no answer to his complaint but the echo of his own voice. The oppressive silence, the sense of isolation from all human association and sympathy is so overwhelming that despair possesses him and leads to the irresistible conclusion of the hypochondriac. Death is desired, but if he comes not like a thief in the night, insidious and certain, then he must be sought with the boldness of a highwayman, rashly, desperately. Thus Faust decides to end the agony of his disappointments. The means he finds at hand, and while mixing the fatal poison he sings with reckless hilarity. But as he lifts the cup to his lips, his purpose is arrested by the soft strains of an Easter hymn, proceeding from a company of peasants on their way to the fields, ending with the refrain,

"Praise ye the Lord! Bless ye our God!"

The name of God seems to inspire him with a frenzy of intolerance, and he fairly shrieks out curses against mankind, against love, joy, prayer, faith, life and death, and ends with the blasphemous invocation, "Infernal king, arise!"

Instantly, in the midst of sulphurous flames and crash of the elements, Mephistopheles appears, in the garb of a gay gentleman of the period, who, with smirking bow, introduces himself. The unexpected apparition startles the Doctor, despite his blasphemous conjuration, seeing which the Evil Genius mockingly questions,

"Are you afraid of me?"

The Doctor answers stoutly in the negative, declares his doubts of the power of Satan, and bids him begone. But the unwelcome visitor remains, and derisively accuses Faust of impoliteness in endeavoring to send him away with so little ceremony, and for neglecting the courtesies due a gentleman who may help him.

Becoming gradually familiar with the presence of the fiend, and curious to learn the object of his visit, Faust inquires what he will do for him?

"Anything in the world!" replies Satan. "All things! But first, what would you have? Abundance of gold?"

"And what can I do with riches?" contemptuously answers the alchemist, who appreciates their vanities.

"Power, then, would you have?"

"No; I would have a treasure which contains all. I wish for youth with all the knowledge I have accumulated!"

"Very well!" replies Mephistopheles; "I can indulge thee even in such caprice, if you would pay the forfeit."

"And what must I give in return?" demands the Doctor, with some misgivings as to his ability to meet the requirements indicated in his tone of voice.

"A mere trifle," replies Satan, reassuringly. "Almost nothing. *Here* shall I be at thy service; but *down yonder* thou shalt be at mine!"

After some hesitation on the part of the Doctor, they agree upon the terms, but as he takes the pen to sign the contract his hand trembles, and he draws back shivering with dread at the probable results of the step he is about to take. Mephistopheles chides

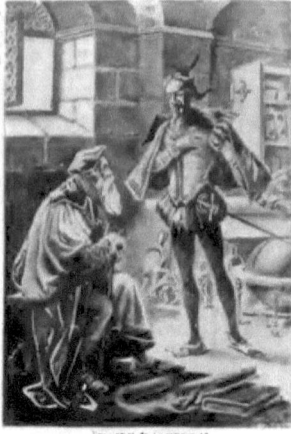

him for his timorousness, and with a commanding gesture causes an apparition of Marguerite at her spinning wheel to appear. Faust is charmed with the glory of the vision. It seems as if heaven has suddenly opened before him, unveiling all that is lovely and beautiful in perfect womanhood.

"Wonderful!" he exclaims. "Oh, beautiful, adorable creature!" and quickly throwing all reluctance to the winds, he eagerly seizes the pen and affixes his signature to the fatal bond that seals his soul to hell, whereupon he receives from the hand of the Evil One a cup containing a magic draught which restores him to young and vigorous life. This done, the two depart, singing the pleasures of youth as they go. Mephistopheles promising his companion that the same day his eyes shall feast upon the matchless beauty of the lovely Marguerite herself.

Scene I. of Act II. represents a fair at Rouen. The city is arrayed in holiday costume. Joy and hilarity prevail without limit or hindrance. Blooming matrons, self-consciously proud in their best attire, gather in chattering groups and merrily discuss their own and their neighbors' affairs. Round-cheeked, bright-eyed maidens troop from every doorway, and flit along the streets, or cluster, like butterflies beneath each shady arbor. Love coyly looks out from mischievous corners of coquettish eyes that flash and sparkle like pearls in the sunshine. Staid citizens, rollicking students, and bearded soldiers converse on politics or business, cast wistful glances at the pretty girls, or drink and shout the glories of war in loud and boisterous songs which impart a glamour of joy to the scene.

In the midst of the revelry, Valentine, a soldier and brother of Marguerite, enters, and in a melancholy song addresses a medallion which hangs about his neck, a gift from his sister, which he wears as a talisman against danger-

FAUST

The soldiers are preparing to march to a distant field of service, and Valentine is sad over the approaching separation from Marguerite, perhaps forever. He is a leader and favorite among his companions, and as they gather about him, he refers to his sister, whom he must so soon leave alone, with no friend to love or care for her.

At this moment Siebel, a friend of Valentine, and secretly a lover of Marguerite, comes forward and declares that he will protect and care for her with the tender love of a brother. Others make similar promises, and the fears of the anxious brother are assuaged in bumpers of wine, drunk with accompaniment of a humorous song by Wagner, a soldier, who is interrupted by the sudden appearance of Mephistopheles. The fiend, assuming the guise of a gentleman, obtrudes upon the company, by the courtesy of a request to be one of them, promising in turn to favor the gathering with a song. This he soon fulfills by rendering "The Golden Calf."

In chorus the students thank the singer, but Valentine observes a sinister appearance in the stranger which excites suspicion of his purposes. Mephistopheles after reading the hand of Wagner forecasting his fate, confesses, to Siebel's inquiry, that he is a sorcerer. Siebel is an honest countryman deeply in love with Marguerite, whose affection is returned, and he therefore shudders when the fiend tells him, "What flowers you would gather shall wither in the grasp. No more bouquets for Marguerite." Valentine angrily demands to know how the fiend has learned her name, to which he is answered.

"Take care, my brave fellow !
Some one I know is destined to kill you."

Mephistopheles now lifts his glass and drinks to the health of all, but not finding the wine to his liking, begs to offer to the company wine from his own cellar. Rapping upon the head of a cask surmounted by a Bacchus, fire flows into his waiting cup and he pledges a draught to Marguerite of Rouet!

Valentine is inflamed with passion by the fiend's toast, and draws his sword to avenge the insult. His action is imitated by the other students, but the sorcerer remains composed, making no defence save to describe a circle with his sword, in which he stands secure against the thrust of mortal. Valentine makes at the fiend, but at the first stroke his sword is shivered in the air, and he sees how futile is all assault against such prince of darkness. Mephistopheles is expelled, however, by the students, who reverse their arms and move towards him, showing the handles of their swords having the sacred sign of the cross.

Faust, who has remained a silent spectator of the scenes enacted, now addresses Mephistopheles, asking where he may meet the lovely child promised in the vision, and demanding to be conducted straightway to her presence. The villagers set up a dance, and the fiend tells Faust to make his choice from among the scores of pretty maids, but he sees none that please him, until presently Marguerite passes, whereupon he advances to offer his arm, but meets with repulse, at which Mephistopheles laughs heartily, and makes sport of his ignorance of love-making. The dance continues by the entire party, singing in chorus, this scene concluding the second act.

Act III.—Scene 1. opens with a splendid representation of the garden attached to Marguerite's house, with Siebel bearing a bouquet and singing a passionate aria of his lady-love, voicing how he shall overcome the sorcerer's evil will. Mephistopheles and Faust enter, who cautiously advance until the fiend, by his arts, causes Siebel to depart after leaving his bouquet at Marguerite's window. Mephistopheles bids Faust abide alone for a few moments while he goes to fetch a treasure which he promises shall far outshine all flowers and of a beauty past believing. While his conductor is gone Faust is seized with a new impulse, a jealous longing, the prompting of sincere infatuation, which rises to the dignity of love, the first time such passion has entered his heart to dispel his misanthropic feelings, and thus he soliloquizes:

"What new emotion penetrates my soul?
Love, a pure and holy love, pervades my being.
Oh, Marguerite behold me at thy feet;"

and sings an exquisite apostrophe to Marguerite's home, "All hail, live innocent."

As the song concludes Mephistopheles reappears bringing a casket of jewels, which he leaves upon the threshold of Marguerite's door, despite the protestations of Faust, who conceives that the sorcerer is designing a sacrifice of innocence. The two withdraw, and there is presented the scene of Marguerite at the spinning wheel, which she trundles while singing a ballad, the folk song entitled "The King of Thule."

When the song is ended Marguerite becomes busy with her thoughts about Faust, the handsome stranger whose advances she had disdained, wondering within herself who he might be, but doubting not that he is some lord. Turning about she discovers the bouquet, and is at no loss to guess by whom it has been left, but almost upon the same instant her eyes fall upon the jewel casket, which immediately absorbs her whole attention.

"Once there was a King of Thule"

With womanly curiosity she craves to open it, and finding the key near by she hesitates but a moment, when raising the lid she is ravished by the gleaming jewels within, so beautiful, rare and scintillant, that she fears it is a dream. But enraptured by the glowing sight she draws from their cushioned receptacles the jewels one by one, and finding a mirror at hand proceeds to invest herself with the rich adornments, and then to admire herself:

"Now, do I look like a coquette?
Ah! I must laugh to see so handsome a face
Reflecting here. Is it I? Is it Marguerite?
Tell me quickly. No! No!
It is not I, nor my poor face.
I see, as it were, a beautiful princess
Whom people salute in the way.
Ah! if he were only here! If he could see me thus!
For now I am a demoiselle,
And he would call me fair."

While Marguerite is thus flattering her own beauty, so splendidly embellished, Dame Martha enters, who with fascinated wonder exclaims, "How beautiful you are: whence came this lovely present?" Marguerite cannot answer, but feels quite sure it is not she who has found such favor. Martha declares the jewels *must* be hers, the gift of some noble lover, and the two are marveling whence the present came, when Mephistopheles appears, with Faust, who by many blandishments presently induces Martha to walk with him a little way, giving opportunity for Faust to speak with Marguerite, whom he first addresses by asking her to continue to wear the jewels. When they are quite alone Marguerite tells him of the sorrows that have fallen like shadows on her soul; that her brother is a soldier, far away; her mother is long dead, and the last consolement of her life, a little sister, tender, and loving none other, has been taken, so that now the world is lonely, and the light of joy extinguished.

Defenceless, yearning for companionship, and craving for some object to love and confide in, Marguerite listens with enraptured ear to the roll expressions and flattering endearments of Faust, the handsome, the youthful, the graceful, and the eloquent pleader. Her modesty is offended by the fervid utterances of Faust; she fears deception, and feels that it is wrong to stay, but yet the story is so sweet, so like sirens' voices, that she cannot turn away. But the hours go by, and gathering shades admonish that time for parting draws near. Faust and Marguerite now sing a beautiful duet, "The Hour is Late, Adieu." When the song is finished Marguerite plucks a flower, and asking a moment to consult its petals, she casts them away one by one, repeating the words, "He loves me; he loves me not." The flower test of his love proves favorable, at which Faust bursts into such rapture of avowal, such eloquence of declaration that Marguerite no longer doubts, and discovers her passion thus:

 Thee would I love, almost worship;
 I love thee; I am thine!
 For thee would I die!
 Now if I am dear to thee,
 Depart! Bid farewell till the morrow!

Answering this confession of the confiding maiden Faust exclaims: "O chaste and holy soul, I obey thee! I depart; but to-morrow,—

 Yet one word. Repeat to me the dear avowal.
 I love thee. Oh, heavenly bliss. Let us depart."

Marguerite now withdraws, and a mocking laugh from Mephistopheles discloses his presence, which irritates Faust, that he should have been heard making his vows, and impatiently he bids the fiend to leave him. Mephistopheles begs him to be more patient, and to deign to listen for a moment to the speech which Marguerite will rehearse to the stars. The sorcerer well understands the emotions and ruling passion of love, for it is he who has inspired this trusting maid. Soon a window of Marguerite's room opens, and believing herself alone she tells her sweet secret to the stars:

 He loves me! He loves me!
 What trouble in my heart!
 The sweet bird sings; the wind murmurs.
 All the voices of nature combine to say
 He loves me! He loves me.
 How heaven smiles on me! I breathe sweet air.
 Rejoice, my heart, in new found love.
 To-morrow! to-morrow! Ah! hasten thy return.
 Oh, my well beloved! Hasten!

Faust is unable to control his joy at thus hearing Marguerite's prayer for his return, and in transport he leaps forward from the bush that concealed him and grasps her hand. Her head falls upon his shoulder, while Mephistopheles laughs with a fiendish glee at the success of his conspiring, as the curtain descends.

Act IV.—Nearly two years are supposed to have elapsed since the passionate scene just described. Faust has not only become master of Marguerite's heart, but, inspired to deeds of deep damnation by his satanic counsellor, he has consummated the imperious wrong that deflowers her maidenhood and leaves her a wreck upon the shores of scorn. The fourth act begins with a street scene in front of Marguerite's home, from which she dejectedly emerges bewailing her shame. Her appearance is greeted by a chorus of girls, who mock her misery, and make sport of the desertion of her lover. Marguerite falls to weeping over her pitiless plight, and to marveling why she should be so persecuted and shunned, when her crime was but the offering of a sinless life upon the altar of supreme affection.

While the poor girl is thus agonizing Siebel appears, and with love unabated he begs to share her griefs, and hurling maledictions upon her seducer, promises to avenge her wrongs. She is moved by his compassion, and the constancy of his love, and thus

FAUST.

with bleeding heart she gives utterance to her unrequited affections, telling how one eve when kneeling by her side the cold hand of Faust suddenly felt her own and that his evil spirit then vanished, since which time she has wept alone, watching by night and day, and counting the hours of his absence. Then with tearful eyes upturned to her faithful lover, she in sorrow speaks of the anguish that torments her soul, for the crime that trusting love has prompted:

> "But not to you, dear Siebel.
> Should I repeat this tale. Your sympathy is sweet.
> The cruel hands of those who slight me
> Cannot shut the doors of God's house
> There, with my child, I go to pray."

Whereupon Marguerite makes her exit to seek consolement at the church, as a company of soldiers enter accompanied by Valentine, who has just returned from the war. Seeing Siebel standing gloomily alone Valentine affectionately embraces and eagerly asks him for news of Marguerite. Embarrassed for answer, he stands mute for a moment, then evasively tells Valentine she has gone into the church. The brother thinking she is there praying for his safe return, asks Siebel to attend him in his house, there to drink a health in honor of his home-coming and victories won afield. Siebel gently refuses and so begs him not to enter that Valentine becomes suspicious of some weighty evil, and demands an explanation. This Siebel cannot give, but implores him in God's name to forgive his sister. Valentine tears himself away and rushes into the house, and Siebel goes to the church with hope to comfort Marguerite.

Faust and Mephistopheles now come upon the scene, the former despising himself for his treachery and confessing still his love, the latter mocking his contrition by a derisive serenade and enacting a contemptuous love scene. While the fiend is thus disporting Valentine emerges and demands to know the cause of his coarse levity. Mephistopheles replies with scornful words, and Faust mentions the name of Marguerite, which so coupled inflames the anger of Valentine who gives a challenge to them both. Mephistopheles banters Faust to accept the brother's defiance, assuring him of victory through the assistance of his magic art. But Faust hesitates, saying

> "Oh, let unhappy!
> Shall I shed the blood of him.
> Loved brother of her I have wronged?"

Valentine is insistent upon fighting, and Faust, forced to defend himself, the two fight with swords until Valentine falls, by mortal thrust. Faust and Mephistopheles hasten away to escape a crowd who being attracted by the noise of the conflict rush onto the stage. Martha is first to discover the wounded man, and Marguerite following perceives that it is Valentine, upon whom she throws herself with cries of anguish. He is appreciative of the sympathies of others, but for his sister he has only execrations. She prays for mercy and beseeches his forgiveness, but to her entreaties he opposes withering words of reviling, declaring that though Heaven may pardon he cannot, and cursing her, as the cause of his death, he expires. Tenderly lifted from her knees by Siebel the bereft Marguerite repairs again to the church to petition for remission of her sins, to find relief from the burden of sorrow and shame that is crushing her soul.

The next scene is one of moving pity, representing Marguerite at prayer before the sacred altar in God's sanctuary. As she piteously cries for mercy, the voice of Mephistopheles is heard.

> "Spirits of evil. Hither! Hither!
> Palsy her tongue for prayer."

at the utterance of which there is heard a chorus of demons, mockingly crying: "Marguerite! Marguerite! Marguerite!"

FAUST 53

She comprehends their cry, and appeals to God, good and merciful, to know if the hour of her punishment has arrived, whereupon the voice of the fiend again rises, speaking to her soul:

"Remember thee of the days that are past,
When wings of bright angels hovered o'er thee.
. . . .
Then God ever listened to thy petitions.
Now in abyss calls to thee. For thee remains,
Naught but endless remorse, anguish eternal,
And night unceasing, hide thee."

Stung and broken by these baleful words proceeding out of the void desecrating the holy temple, seeing no man, but feeling a fresh torment in her soul, she agonizingly lifts her eyes to heaven, petitioning:

"Oh, God! What voice thus calls in the darkness?
What thick shadows descend upon my soul?"

But no answer of God is heard in reply, only that of the fiend, who hushes even a choral of church worshipers, to mock her supplications and expose the opening gates of hell to receive her damned spirit. Thus overwhelmed, a prey to demons, her mind dethroned by the torment, she rushes from the church a maniac. Faust now appears, who though a slave to Satan, through the compact that gave him youth, has still some lingering compassion; nor has his love for Marguerite been entirely extinguished. In shame and fear he cries, "My blood chills within me;" therefore to steep his soul more deeply in the guilt of hell, Mephistopheles gives to Faust a cup filled with a beverage that compels forgetfulness of evils past and conjures voluptuous visions. This Faust eagerly drinks, and his soul becomes enchanted with "dreams serene, forgetting virtue, faith and heaven," and pictures of goddesses of ravishing beauty, luring on to fields abloom with death. But these intoxicating witcheries are not all that beguile Faust, for amidst them all he beholds another vision: that of the pale, soul-anguished Marguerite, about whose neck he discovers a thin red line like the cut of an axe, and to Mephistopheles he cries: "I must see her. Come, I will it!"

Thereupon appears a troop of imps who sing in chorus, while stirring a hell broth:

"One, two, three : count to thirteen !
Peasants are kings ; kings are common men.
Stir the broth,—the fire, in flames blue and red.
Poison wine distill ! 'Tis just the drink for the dead !"

As the imps stir and sing, a procession of dead,—lost souls surrendered to Mephistopheles as the price for earthly preferments,—pass by, which terrible scene of woe concludes the fourth act.

In Gounod's interpretations of Goethe's story, one of the most powerful scenes is omitted, viz : the riot and rout at the convocation of witches, in the Brocken, on "Walpurgis Night." This revel of the Sabbat is made a special feature of Boito's opera, "Mephistopheles," who introduces it as a thrilling tableau to emphasize the satanic pronouncement which Mephistopheles delivers to Marguerite, "Thou art cursed forever; the abyss yawns to receive thee," which so shocks the hopeless girl that she falls unconscious, to revive in ravening madness, a damned soul with distempered mind

Act V—During the interval between Acts IV. and V. Marguerite, in her maniacal frenzy, has strangled her child, and Act V. therefore opens with a prison scene, showing Marguerite, condemned to death, lying in chains upon a pallet of straw. The prison guard is asleep, as Faust and Mephistopheles enter, coming to liberate Marguerite, for remorse has driven Faust to demand the fiend's assistance, under threat to break his contract. The scaffold has been prepared and haste is necessary, since on the morrow morn the execution is appointed. Mephistopheles says he will watch without, while Faust enters the prison to apprise Marguerite of the help at hand. Gaining access to the cell Faust approaches the sleeping girl and on bended knee gives utterance to his agony of repentance.

"My heart is penetrated with sorrow.
Oh, torture! Oh, source of eternal regret.
This gentle creature in the depths of a prison!
Despair has dethroned her reason.
Her poor child. O God! destroyed!
Destroyed by thy hand, Marguerite!"

The sound of Faust's voice arouses the sleeping girl, who recognizing that it is he who laments, rejoices with bounding heart and implores him to save her from the fiends. Suddenly she fancies herself once more the pure, coyish girl whom Faust accosted on her way from church, when first the holy flame of love was lighted in her heart. She forgets the chains, the fatal sentence, and her still trusting, loyal heart, swelling with a boundless love, would make further sacrifices to prove her devotion. At the sound of his voice she revives as one quaffing immortal elixir, and in ecstasy she cries:

"Now am I free. He is here. It is his voice.
Fetters, death, have no terrors for me.
Thou hast found me. Thou hast returned."

Then reverting to other days, when first they met, Marguerite pathetically reminds Faust of the place and time when he awoke in her the passion that wrought her undoing, when she with such reserve as masks a maiden's heart did blush objection to his offered arm. But wrung by remorse, distracted by fear, Faust seeks to interrupt her passionate utterances and make her sensible to the danger of delay. He implores her to seize the opportunity of escape, to fly with him to safety, but Marguerite would stay to enjoy the bliss of being encircled by the arms of her recreant but now sorrowing lover. The scene is most affecting, and its closing leaves the auditor flooded with tears of sympathy. Mephistopheles exhorts Faust to flee, and he in turn begs the demented girl to come with him, but the voice of the demon serves to renew her fears, and she begs her lover to save her, not from the executioner, but from the burning gaze of the prince of darkness. To God also she offers her supplications for protection, that "angels radiant may bear her soul to heaven." As Marguerite is praying the morning breaks and Faust implores her to fly with him ere the guard awakens and the executioners approach, but she cannot be aroused; a dreadful vision rises before her; it is her own reflection, the wraith of her crime: 'Wherefore this menacing look? Wherefore these hands red with blood? Go! I abhor thee!" and with these last words she falls and expires as Mephistopheles exclaims, "Judged!"

The prison suddenly becomes radiant, and a host of angels pour in to receive the ransomed soul of Marguerite, as Faust, remorseful, expels Mephistopheles, who sinks into hell with a cry of baffled rage.

A SKETCH OF MASCAGNI.

PIETRO MASCAGNI, whose fame was perhaps more suddenly acquired than that of any other composer, was born in Leghorn, Italy, December 7, 1863, the son of a baker, who though almost poor had an ambition to make a lawyer of Pietro, and husbanded his slender means to that end. But the boy had no inclination for the bar, all his tastes being musical; and disregarding parental objections, he secretly began a course of music under Soffredini, which he continued until discovery by his father compelled a return to his law-books. Pietro was in great distress for a time, until his uncle, Stefano, relieved his disappointment by persuading his father to allow him to take the youth to his own house. The uncle thereafter not only encouraged Pietro, but also provided him with the means for pursuing his musical studies, besides placing a piano at his disposal for daily practice. Soffredini continued to act as the boy's teacher, and very soon had the satisfaction of proving to the father that Pietro had remarkable talent, which, properly directed, promised to make him famous as a musician, a prophecy that was not long of fulfillment.

Two years after becoming a pupil of Soffredini, Pietro made his initial attempts at composition, producing a symphony in C minor, that was rendered in 1879, with much credit to the author. Two years later he composed a cantata ("In Filanda"), and a hymn ("To Joy"), both of which were so successful that he attracted the attention and won the favor of Count Larderell, who generously offered to defray the expenses of the promising young musician through a course at the Conservatory at Milan. Pietro was transported with delight at this great kindness, and applied himself with much diligence at the Conservatory for almost one year, but before graduating he was persuaded from his studies by a flattering offer made to him by the manager of an operatic troupe to become musical director of the company. Under this engagement he traveled for some time in Italy, and until the company disbanded, because of ill fortune, leaving him sick and penniless in Naples. In this desperate condition, when hope and life seemed almost spent, he fell under the care of a handsome young lady, who nursed him back to health, and at the same time inspired him with the passion of love as well as of gratitude, which led to proposal and marriage, though at the time he was poorly prepared to assume the responsibilities of a benedict, being entirely without financial means.

Leaving Naples, Mascagni became a teacher of music in various cities of Italy, but his reward was so small that he was many times upon the borders of despair, and became cynical and morbid. In the hour of his deepest discouragement, by chance he saw in a newspaper an announcement by Sonzogno, a large music publisher, offering prizes for the three best one-act operas, which were required to be complete, in libretto and score, and submitted in a fortnight from the date that he discovered the advertisement. No time, therefore, must be lost. In a moment he determined to contest for the prize. "He went home to his piano," says Cosmopolite, in *Town Topics*, "and built his castle in the air. He built it up of harmonious sixths and dissonant sevenths, of wandering melodies, of tumbling arpeggios, of scampering scales; he drew it up with the strings of violins and violas; he lit it with the trills of clarionets and flutes; he softened it with the curves of the woman-voiced hautbois; and the splash of harps, like fountains, rose and fell in its courts. Then he stole out and went to the huge, solid palaces where the great musicians live with their fame. He took bars and bricks from Verdi's castle of melodies; he took tall columns of harmony from Gounod's gothic temples; he dragged mosaics and embroidery from Massenet's Indian palace of Lahore; he stole wreaths of rhythmic dances from the vault where Bizet, sullen in his posthumous glory, lies asleep. Then he found gems and jewels of street songs in the huts of Sicilian peasantry—songs, born in the sulphur mines, of tears

Pietro Mascagni.

and starvation. All this he carried back to his palace of sound, his castle in the air, which rose like a stately dream under his thin fingers. And over it he flung the strong protecting roof of Verga's love story.

"'Cavalleria Rusticana' was produced. Mascagni, in a borrowed dress-suit, saw the arch of his triumph ascend and curve above his disheveled head. When Sonzogno kissed him, he knew it was not the impresario's little black moustache alone that brushed his face; it was Fortuna's fluttering curl. He grasped it, he wound it round his eager hand, and dragged the goddess from her wheel away across Europe, across the world, away after his singing caprice."

His reputation was established with the suddenness of an electric shock, and that, too, by a one-act opera, the music of which he composed in the remarkably short time of one week. "Cavalleria Rusticana" of course received the first prize, and when it was produced in Rome, the audience became a very whirlwind of enthusiasm, not only demanding that the composer appear before the curtain, but continuing their plaudits until he had responded no less than twenty times.

A year after "Cavalleria Rusticana" was given to the public, Mascagni produced "L' Amico Fritz," followed quickly by "I Rantzau," neither of which fulfilled expectation. In 1895 appeared two more of his operas, "Guglielmo Ratcliff" and "Silvano," which had their presentations at Milan, followed by "Zanetto" in 1896, and by "Isis" in 1898, the latter a pronounced success; but though he has produced no other opera equaling in popularity the one which apparently cost him the least time, Mascagni is unquestionably a man of genius, from whom the public may confidently expect great things. At this time, he holds the position of director of the Rossini Conservatory at Pesaro, Italy, enjoying the honors that have been conferred upon him by great persons and societies, and the profound admiration of the people among whom he lives.

It was my fortune and pleasure in June, 1897, to visit Mascagni at his home in Pesaro, which is a town of some 13,000 inhabitants, on the Adriatic Sea, 200 miles south of Venice. The place has some claim to renown, not so much for its silk-spinning, iron founding, and tanneries, which are its chief industries, as for its antiquity and musical associations. It was the home of more than one great poet in the time of Roman predominance, and became famous as the birthplace of Rossini, who upon his death, in 1868, left his fortune, by will, for the founding of a musical lyceum in the city. Much earlier, however, was his love for Pesaro manifested, for in 1818, by his efforts, the Rossini Theatre was opened, which after a fitful career, chiefly of embarrassments, was closed and is now in a condition of sad decay. The Lyceum, better known as the Rossini Conservatory, was so well endowed that it continues in a flourishing state, greatly popularized by the appointment of so worthy a successor as Mascagni to be chief director. At the time of my visit Mascagni was very busy directing a band of sixty instruments, rehearsing for a concert to be given three days later, and being admitted as a privileged auditor, my opportunity was perfect to observe the composer in his role of leadership.

Upon invitation I also met his family, consisting of a remarkably amiable wife and two very bright children, with whom I conversed at length through their English governess. Mascagni is now possessor of a comfortable competence, and is in receipt of a large income, but economical habits, acquired through the harsh necessities of his earlier years, prompts him to live in a modest way, though his hospitalities are bountiful. To my surprise I found that his living quarters are on the fourth floor of a section of the Lyceum Building, and as lifts, or elevators, are quite unknown in Pesaro, the only means of reaching them are by flights of winding staircases. The air is pure and the light is excellent when the home of this great composer is reached, and his manner of entertainment is so intellectual and cordial that my hard climb was delightfully compensated. In my conversations I repeated some of the stories (current especially in America), and anecdotes associated with his peripatetic career as a minstrel, and of incidents immediately preceding his achievement of fame. Both he and his wife laughed heartily at my repeating a widely-circulated report to the effect that upon the completion of "Cavalleria Rusticana" he was so illy satisfied with his work that in a rage of vexation he tossed it into the fire, from which the manuscript was timely rescued by his more appreciative wife. They both declared that, so far from being disappointed with the composition, they had from the beginning implicit confidence in its success, and their concern arose alone from the fact that being very poor and without influence they doubted their fortune of ever securing a public representation of the opera.

Mascagni is content to live plainly, and his sensible wife, equally devoted as a mother, assumes the household responsibilities with perfect satisfaction; but both are devoted to music, whose lives are united by identical ambitions, and whose home is the echo cave of song. Being yet young and aspiring, Mascagni looks towards the future with large expectations, and as he is an indefatigable worker in his chosen field, with opportunities of submitting his creations now to not only a thoroughly appreciative, but to an almost idolizing public, a belief in his ability to produce a composition superior to "Cavalleria" is very generally shared.

Cavalleria Rusticana

AFTER THE ORIGINAL PAINTING BY WILLIAM ST LEFFWICH DODGE

TURIDDU — "*One kiss, dear mother, and yet another!*
    Farewell now! If I return not, be a mother to my Santa."

Scene XI

CAVALLERIA RUSTICANA.

(RUSTIC CHIVALRY.)

Music by Pietro Mascagni.——Words by Signori Targioni-Tozetti and Menasci.

CAVALLERIA RUSTICANA is one of the shortest of all the popular operas, and is played in one act and twelve scenes. Its first performance occurred on the 20th of May, 1890, in the Constanzi Theatre at Rome, with Gemma Bellinconi and Roberto Stagno in the two principal roles. So favorable was the reception of the opera that it was soon produced in all the principal cities of Europe, and on the 9th of September, 1891, it had its first American representation in the city of Philadelphia, on which occasion Mme. Kronold took the part of Santuzza, Miss Campbell that of Lola, Guille appearing as Turiddu, Del Puente as Alfio, and Jennie Teal as Lucia. The rapidly shifting incidents of the story of "Cavalleria Rusticana" sustain an unflagging interest; while the motive of the piece, resting as it does upon the master-passions of love and jealousy, can never fail to touch the hearts of men and women, who see in the mimic representation an illustration of the same feelings and sentiments that have at various times swayed and shaped their own destinies.

The scene of the story is laid in a country village of the Island of Sicily. Turiddu, the hero, son of Lucia, and the handsomest youth of the village, loves the beautiful dark-eyed Lola, who reciprocates his tender sentiment with all the ardor and intensity of her warm southern nature. They have grown up together as children; together their little feet have pattered along the pebbly beach; hand in hand they have gathered the bright flowers and mellow fruits of their sunny clime, and in the course of this intimate and pleasant association the great mystery of the divine passion has flashed from soul to soul through glances of mutual tenderness. Thus they grew from infancy to childhood, and from childhood to youth, gliding lovingly, trustingly, tenderly, along the placid stream of early life, bordered on either side with scented forests and nodding flowers that blushed and smiled in happy unison with these two innocent and confiding hearts. No thought of coming evil disturbed their delightful anticipations. They appeared to have been created for each other, and composed a little world of their own, whose metes and bounds were fixed only by the law of their love.

But an awakening from rapturous dreams came with the rudeness of a sudden shock. One day in the early autumn, when the trees and hillsides had just begun to robe themselves in demure colors of a mild southern winter, the roll of the conscription officer's drum was heard in the village, and the handsome Turiddu was one among the first to be drawn for service in distant camps and upon hostile fields. The pang of parting was the first sorrow that had come to these loving hearts, but with the buoyancy and hopefulness of youth, they looked forward to an ending of the term of martial duty, when they should be again united in their sweet companionship, and so they kissed, and embraced, and parted.

Turiddu went to the wars, to experiences and excitements of camp life, where he was transformed by the polishing art of military drill from a good-looking, merry-faced country boy, into an erect, graceful and manly youth. No letters passed between these lovers to encourage and foster the tender flame of their devotion, and it was but seldom that they heard from one another through the chance opportunity of some passing messenger; for they were but ignorant country people, unaccustomed to the mysteries of composition; and the exactions of the military rules to which Turiddu was subjected, gave no opportunity, during his entire service, for the young lovers to enjoy personal intercourse. Yet, through the slow dragging length of all these weary years, Turiddu remained true to the sweetheart of his boyhood. Her beautiful image was enshrined in the most sacred recesses of his soul, and amid all the stirring scenes of his soldier-life it departed not from his conscious recollection. The memory of her maidenly coyness, her modest demeanor, and the light of love that kindled ever for him in her beautiful eyes, was the inspiration of his being, and the guardian angel that led him constantly in the path of truth and noble manliness.

Lola, more beautiful than any other maid of the village, and coquettish as she was charming, became the object of many amorous swains, whose attentions were in no wise disdainful, and whose court she encouraged. So long had her lover been absent, that the flame of her passion subsided, and other comely youths made her forget the vow she had made when Turiddu was conscripted. But those who were of fluent speech, to tell their admiration by word and song, which might win so fair a lady, were poor of purse, and flattery had made Lola ambitious to become the bride of one who was able to gratify her vanity for fine things. In the village there was only one such, Alfio, a carter, muscular, coarse, and clownish, but withal so provident that his fortune appeared large by comparison with the small possessions of all other suitors. His voice, too, was strong, and he sang of his wealth, and of his position, so that when he wooed Lola she lent a rapt ear to his proposals, even though her heart was unresponsive. And so the vain maid dismissed all thought of her soldier sweetheart and married Alfio, the carter, who with pride provided the captured bird with a pretty cage, esteeming himself the most fortunate of mortals and the happiest of men.

A year, perhaps two, or more, had passed since Turiddu joined the army; little had been heard of him, and his name was no longer spoken by the villagers. But the term of his enforced service at length expired and with nimble feet he hurried away towards his home, his heart filled with blissful anticipations and pictures of Lola, whom he would soon make his wife. No jealous dread disturbed his reveries, for faithful himself he gave implicit confidence to the girl he loved. His home-coming was little heralded, for he was only a poor soldier; but when the dreadful news of Lola's faithless act reached his ears Turiddu felt all the grief that heart of king is capable. Lowly of origin yet his pride was deeply touched, and his feelings he therefore dissembled by paying his addresses to another girl of the village, Santuzza, for whom, however, his love was impure.

Secretly, Turiddu fed the unlawful flame which burned for Lola, and sought for opportunity to test the permanence of her affections, for love repressed his pride and made him slave to forbidden purpose. Pursuit of his resolve to yet win the heart of Lola made Turiddu bold, nor were his endeavors futile, for the fickle wife quickly grew tired of her coarse and unlovable husband, and welcomed the return of Turiddu's devotions with such manifestations of satisfaction that her conduct soon became the subject of village gossip, and of Alfio's jealous rage. These are the events that precede the operatic drama.

The story upon which Mascagni founded his most popular opera is a Sicilian tale beautifully told by Giovanni Verga, familiar to every Italian, but not translated, to my knowledge, into English. While dealing with the master passion, and picturing pronounced traits of human nature by realistic description, the novelist's beads of sentiment are coarsely strung, and in some respects the story would be positively shocking but for the fact that the actors belong to a substratum of life where environment is vulgar, if not squalid. It is to Mascagni's sublime art that we owe redemption of the plot, for he has, by witchery of melodic composition, transformed an indecorous tale into an ear-pleasing and effective opera, which gave him almost instant fame throughout both Europe and America.

The lyric action begins with a song by Turiddu praising the beauty of Lola and declaring that if heaven should open its gates to receive him he would not enter if Lola were not there to greet him. This is sung before the curtain rises, but immediately it is concluded a scene is disclosed that represents a village square with Mother Lucia's dwelling and an inn on the left and a small church on the right. It is early Easter morning and as the bell rings, calling to service, a crowd of peasant people and villagers appear and enter the church, while a chorus of female voices is heard behind the scene singing of vernal beauties and the world's gladness for return of the season when lovers plight their vows. After thus singing, the women come upon the stage and a chorus of male voices is heard behind the scenes, expressing joy for resting time, under cooling shades after the toil of day is done, and praising the fair ones whose spinning wheels and merry voices have enraptured them. As the men enter, the women continue their song, admonishing that as this is "Love's

CAVALLERIA RUSTICANA

happy hour," when thoughts of the Blessed Virgin should fill all hearts; when charity for the faults of others, and love for all should bless our lives; and thus singing all leave the stage to attend mass.

Scene II.—While the market square is still and deserted, Santuzza, a peasant girl, enters and hesitatingly advancing to the door of Lucia's (Turiddu's mother) dwelling, knocks thereon. The summons is promptly answered and Santuzza, with halting speech, eagerly asks, "Tell me, Mother Lucia, where is thy son?" Lucia is both angered and surprised by the inquiry. She has suspected the relations that have for some time existed between Santuzza and her son, and has been shamed by it, so with ill-concealed anger she answers:

"My son? Why have you come to see Turiddu? I know not! I know not! I brook no quarrels."

Santuzza is grief-stricken by Lucia's angry tone and by her refusal to answer a question which is preferred in sorrowful accents that might well excite sympathy; reflecting a moment how she may gain the mother's pity, Santuzza in tears beseeches:

> "Mother Lucia, I pray you heed my weeping;
> Do unto me as Christ did to the Magdalen.
> Tell me, in pity's name,
> Where hides Turiddu?"

As the girl lies sobbing at her feet Lucia's compassion is aroused, and feelingly she answers that he has gone to Francofonte to fetch wine. This, Santuzza declares, cannot be true, for Turiddu was seen in the village on the evening before, which statement fills the mother with anxiety, for her son has not come home. With the hope of learning more, Lucia invites Santuzza into her house, which the girl declines because it is forbidden, since for her sin she has been excommunicated. This serves to increase the fears of Lucia, who eagerly demands, "What evil have you of my son to tell me?"

Santuzza would speak, but as she utters, "In my heart what torture," she is interrupted by the sound of cracking whip and jingling bells behind the scene, and the appearance of a crowd of women singing in chorus, followed by Alfio.

Scene III, thus introduced, presents Alfio, who sings merrily of his sturdy steed, and his jolly trade, and of Lola whose love enthralls him. A number of women of the chorus now pass into the church while others scatter to their homes, leaving Alfio, Lucia, and Santuzza alone together. Lucia compliments Alfio upon his cheerful disposition, to which he hastily acknowledges by asking if she has any left of the excellent wine for which she is famous. She thereupon tells him that her store is quite exhausted, but that Turiddu has gone away to buy more. This Alfio denies, saying, "Nay, nay; he is here! This very morn I saw him—lingering near my cottage." Lucia, alarmed, is upon the point of expressing her astonishment when Santuzza abruptly bids her be silent. Alfio then takes his leave, not discovering the women's trepidation, telling them to hasten into the church, to their devotions. As Alfio disappears there is heard the chant of priests and the devotees' responses, and other worshipers come hurrying towards the church door, joining their voices in the Easter Carols.

> "Queen of heaven, our grief is ended,
> He whom thy boundless love defended,
> From the tomb is now ascended—
> Is ascended as He promised. Hallelujah!"

Two choruses, one from the church and one from the market square, sing orisons to the risen Lord, after which all those on the outside enter, save Santuzza and Lucia, who, in Scene IV, continue their interview, interrupted by the appearance of Alfio. Lucia asks Santuzza why she so earnestly commanded her to be silent when she was speaking with Alfio; suspicious, yet not fully advised, of the new relations which Turiddu has formed; mindless that the old love has been cast off for a new, or that in the mutations which are so common to youth, Turiddu has been lured, by opportunities, to again offer his heart to that first beloved who is now unworthy to receive it. Santuzza, a picture of grief, bowed by her sense of shame and bitter humiliation, thus answers the inquiring Lucia:

"Well do you know, good mother, when to the war he departed
Turiddu gave to Lola a pledge of love true hearted;
But returning to find her wedded he gladly,
To extinguish the flame that burned madly,
Came to love me as I loved him. She, coveting my treasure,
And burning with fell displeasure,
Enticed him from me.
Robbed of my maidenhood, my sorrow is deep,
She and Turiddu love again. For this I weep."

This exposure of shame horrifies Lucia, who begs Santuzza to seek the church, there to pray for mercy and remission, but the hapless girl has been cast out and she therefore begs Lucia, whose soul is pure, to implore God to save her, promising to see Turiddu and upon her knees to beseech him once more to be faithful. Lucia is somewhat consoled by the suppliant's devotion, and calling upon the Blessed Virgin to help her, she enters the church to pray.

Scene V is the most dramatic of the opera. Santuzza is alone, before the church door, as Turiddu enters and with supercilious air tells her it is Easter and asks if she is going to church. Santuzza, trembling with excitement, admits she has come here with the hope of meeting him, for she has much of importance to speak of. Turiddu tries to avoid her, but so insistent is she that he shall hear her, that she questions him of things that he cannot refuse to answer. She disputes his assertion that he has been to Francofonte for wine, and boldly declares that he was seen lurking about Lola's house last night. He denounces her as a spy upon his movements, but she resents this charge by telling him that it is Alfio who reports that he saw him near his cottage, and, moreover, will declare it through the town till scandal shall be upon him. Turiddu is both angered and alarmed by Santuzza's accusations, and terrifies her by asking if it be her wish that Alfio should kill him! When she appeals to him not to charge her with such desire he rudely commands her to leave him, nor attempt to soothe out of pity his rising indignation. Santuzza, cautious not to offend, employs all artifices of speech to obtain from him an admission of his feelings, and asks if he does not really love Lola. He denies his affections, but with such confusion that his words belie him, and believing Turiddu to be lost to her, and no longer able to control her resentments, she reviles him as a recreant, and Lola as a guilty wretch who, being wedded, would yet commit the crime of enticing his love from her.

"Silence, Santuzza! I refuse to be a slave to thy jealous exactions," he thus upbraids her, to which she replies in broken utterances:

"Loving thee I languish until I die with anguish."

"Strike me! Shun me! Still I adore
And bow down before thee.
Loving thee I languish
Until I die with anguish."

Scene VI.—The quarrel is interrupted by the voice of Lola, behind the scenes, who approaches singing:

"My king of roses, no radiant angel stands
So bright in heaven lands
As he, my king of roses."

Suddenly coming upon the couple, she attempts to conceal her embarrassment by affecting surprise, saying, "Ah! Turiddu! Have you seen Alfio?" "No," answers the discomfited lover. "I have not seen him, having only this moment come to the market place." "Then," answers she, "he may have waited to see the blacksmith; but I must not tarry."

CAVALLERIA RUSTICANA

Casting a malicious glance at Santuzza, she superciliously inquires, "Are you attending church service out of doors?" Turiddu, with much confusion, attempts to explain that Santuzza has paused a moment to pass a compliment, whereupon the lorn girl interrupts: "Yes, I came to tell him that this is Easter Day, when the Lord beholds all actions." To this sharp answer Lola can make no approving reply, so with hope of avoiding a quarrel she asks, "Are you not going to mass?" With vehemence Santuzza replies, "Not I! None should go save those who know they have not sinned." Lola submissively acknowledges the truth of Santuzza's saying. To prevent further unpleasant controversy between the two women, Turiddu would leave, asking Lola to accompany him, but with show of jealousy she refuses, ironically bidding him remain with Santuzza, while she abruptly turns away, leaving her blessings with the couple, and enters the church.

Scene VII.—Santuzza and Turiddu thus left alone resume their recriminations, he angrily berating, and she seeking to conciliate his wrath. He abuses her for speaking so offensively to Lola, to which she answers by cold and threatening words, until stung to desperate desire to be rid of her he utters a malediction, bidding her go forever from him. These words of hateful scorn wound the poor girl beyond cure, and in wailing tones she exclaims:

> "My heart is broken. Turiddu, heed me! Remain, oh, remain!
> Do not leave me, though in deepest anguish
> I know you will deceive me.
> Do not forsake me, nor forsake me of your favor.
> Lo! here thy Santuzza weeping implores thee.
> How canst thou scorn the maid who adores thee,
> Hapless Santuzza?"

This frantic appeal only increases the anger of the false lover who, in passionate tones, commands her to be gone!

"Go! it is my sentence; and mistake me not, for vain is repentance after your insults."

With fury in her eyes, Santuzza threateningly advances towards him, shouting, "Braggart! what will you?" Thus defied, Turiddu forgets his manhood, and seizing the girl, throws her violently upon the ground, shouting, "Thus I reward you in my anger!" and then hurries into the church, followed by Santuzza's imprecations, "May all misfortune smite thee, miserable betrayer!"

Scene VIII.—As Turiddu disappears, Alfio comes upon the scene, whom Santuzza greets with attempt at composure, which, however, she is not able to perfectly simulate. With trembling voice she tells him that God must have sent him to her at this moment when suffering most from wrongs of one she has loved. Alfio does not appear to notice her agitation and asks, "At what point is the service?" "It is almost over," she answers. "But I tell you Lola has gone with Turiddu!" Affecting surprise, he asks, "What is your meaning?" Impatient that Alfio does not comprehend her warning, she plainly tells him how he is being deceived by a faithless wife and perfidious lover; that while he his labors are pursuing, his wife, mindless of her duties, is flagrantly entertaining Turiddu, who even now is with her, profaning the church with their guilty presence, performing their evil deeds in the face of God!

Stupefied by the girl's blunt charges, Alfio pitifully asks, "Ah, in the name of Heaven, what say you, Santuzza?"

"The very truth," she answers, "for my lover has betrayed me, and it was Lola, your wife, who enticed him from me!"

Alfio is slow to believe such infamous accusation, half suspecting that

some jealous rage inspires her utterance, and with a scowl of anger he tells her, if she wrongs his wife by lying words that he will punish her as her crime deserves. Santuzza so earnestly declares the truth of what she has told that Alfio, after a pause, expresses his gratitude for the information. Santuzza exhibits a tinge of remorse for having betrayed so shameful a secret, but Alfio is now keenly sensitive of the disgrace which has been brought upon him through his wife's erring, and with many a dire threat he promises to be avenged upon the despoiler of his home before the day expires.

Scene IX.—The gem of the opera, known as the intermezzo, by which "Cavalleria Rusticana" became famous, is played as a prelude to the succeeding scene. It is no flattery to pronounce this interlude one of the most exquisite and expressive compositions ever set to stringed instruments. It has about it enough of the weird to fascinate, and of tuneful charm to stir the soul. The plot is prosaic, and often dull, with painful interrogation, but Mascagni has covered it so deeply with jewels of instrumentation that the opera is a blaze of splendor, under which the libretto is entirely hidden. His intermezzo is a sublime expression of musical poesy, an embodied inspiration of melody, strains caught, like Schubert and Mozart, from the spheres, that rise heavenward, waving and fading until they expire, leaving a sweet vision for contemplation.

As the intermezzo ceases crowds are seen leaving the church, and Lucia crosses the square and enters the inn. A group of men pause on the scene and sing of their duty to hasten home to join their wives, and a chorus of women take up the strain as it falls, tuning their voices to similar sentiments. Turiddu and Lola now appear, coming from opposite directions, and as she is about to pass without recognition, he asks why she does not stop to speak to him. When Lola answers that she must not delay, since she has not yet found Alfio, Turiddu tells her not to worry, for she will certainly see him soon enough. Speaking then to the chorus of men and women he invites them all to join him at the bar of the inn in a glass of wine. The groups gladly accept, and gather about the tables, where, as their cups are filled, Turiddu sings a praise of wine:

"They make that flow before one across goes."

"Hail the red wine richly flowing,
In our cups so brightly glowing,
Love's happy smiles our holiday will bless.
Hail, sweet wine, that laughs in bubbles;
That drowns in joy our sorest troubles;
That eases pangs by forgetfulness."

When his song is concluded, Turiddu raises his cup and drinks to the love of Lola, who in turn gives a compliment to Turiddu. The chorus then sings the verse just rendered by Turiddu, at which juncture Alfio enters.

Scene X.—Alfio cordially greets the company, which rise from their tables, as Turiddu pours a glass of wine and presents it as an evidence of their cordial welcome. Alfio, scowling and defiant, refuses to accept wine from the hands of the violator of his honor, who, he charges, may be treacherous enough to poison the draught. Turiddu throws away the wine and sneeringly replies, "Oh, suit your pleasure!" Lola observes the gathering clouds that portend a storm of anger, and anxiously inquires the meaning of this hostile exhibition! Many women of the company also perceive that serious trouble is imminent, and after excitedly consulting a moment together they approach Lola and ask her to leave the place. She refuses, and the women depart, leaving her alone with Alfio and Turiddu.

With defiant air Turiddu turns towards Alfio, saying, "Have you any words to speak to me?" When Alfio sullenly answers that he has no wish to bandy words, and by threatening looks gives intimation that he prefers

CAVALLERIA RUSTICANA.

THE DUEL BETWEEN ALFIO AND TURIDDU

action, Turiddu tells him, whatever he would demand, satisfaction for his wounded honor if he wishes, that he will find him ready to accord it.

"Do you mean at this moment?" asks Alfio. "Aye," responds Turiddu, "upon the instant," and embracing him he bites Alfio's right ear. This was formerly a Sicilian custom of giving a challenge, a form which in the country districts of the island is still occasionally observed.

Preserving an imperturbable mien Alfio promptly accepts the challenge, and remains unmoved to await what may follow. Turiddu now manifests some compunction, but warningly threatens:

"Neighbor Alfio, I confess that I have deeply wronged you; so guilty have I acted that a villain's death I deserve; but I warn you, that if I perish at your hands, poor Santuzza, whom I swore to marry, being left without a lover, or one to succor, will avenge me by striking a dagger into your heart."

This confession and solemn caution gives no alarm to Alfio, whose passion has stirred him to desperate resolution, and he coolly tells Turiddu he will wait his coming behind the orchard wall.

Scene XI.—In the following scene occurs the interview between Turiddu and his mother, one of the most pathetic incidents of the story. As Lucia appears Turiddu, affecting a jocund demeanor, tells her so much wine he has been drinking that excited he must take a stroll to remove its effects; but as if just realizing what may be the result of his fight with Alfio, the lusty and vengeful carter, whose strength is fortified by right, Turiddu, somewhat dejectedly, addresses Lucia: "Before I go, mother, may I crave your blessing, such as you gave me when I became a soldier? And listen, mother, if I return not again I adjure you, fondest parent, be a mother to Santuzza, for I have sworn to cherish and to make her my wife. It may be you, only, who can now protect her."

Alarmed by his words, conceiving that therein lies some dreadful foreboding, Lucia begs her son to explain his strange speech, but Turiddu nonchalantly answers, "It is nothing! Wine has filled my brain with its disturbing vapors, and I babble without meaning." But again he relapses into melancholy, exclaiming, "Oh, pray that God may forgive me! One kiss, dearest mother, and yet another. I must now say farewell. Remember, though, again I charge you, if I come no more, be thou a mother to Santuzza." Thus beseeching, Turiddu departs to meet Alfio in a deadly duel with daggers behind the orchard wall.

Scene XII.—Lucia, in great state of dread, stands looking after the retreating form of her son, when Santuzza enters, and rushing to the trembling woman throws her arms about her neck crying. "Mother Lucia!" At this moment a large crowd of villagers come upon the stage eagerly inquiring one of another what news of Alfio! of Turiddu! of Lola! for the report of an impending conflict has swiftly sped among the people. While Lucia and Santuzza are thus clasped in each other's arms, and the

"Neighbor Turiddu has been murdered!"

CAVALLERIA RUSTICANA

Lucia Faints and Santuzza Falls.

crowd is exhibiting agitation, a woman comes running frantically, hysterically crying, "Neighbor Turiddu has been murdered!" The first herald of this terrible news is followed quickly by others, shouting and crying confirmation of the report, which falls with such sudden horror upon the startled senses of Lucia that, for a moment, she stands in mute amazement, unable to realize the full import of the dreadful tidings. When she comprehends, in all its awful earnestness, that Turiddu has been slain, her worn face, of an anxious mother becomes pathetic in its exhibition of unutterable grief, and fainting, she is borne away by a chorus of women sympathizers. Santuzza, broken-hearted by her rejection and shame, but constant to the end to the man whose perfidy, after working so much misery, has at last found its mortal punishment, gazes about her in wild despair, until the measure of her loneliness becomes revealed by the desertion of all about her, the loss of lover, foster-mother and friends, and curse of the church that brands her an outcast, when she, too, swoons, as the curtain falls upon the story of the village tragedy.

In the operatic representations of Verger's tale the duel scene between Turiddu and Alfio is not shown, an omission which is much remarked upon, as neglect to employ such an effective ante-climax as a spirited encounter with knives, after the Sicilian fashion, would afford, robs the conclusion of a great part of the impressive influence of previous situations, and gives a sense of incompleteness to the opera. Such curtailment is the more noticeable and less defensible because the drama is presented with few climaxes and many scenes, tending sometimes to weary an audience and to make the interest dependent almost entirely upon the music. The instrumentation, however, is of such flexible and always brilliant character that the purely dramatic features are reduced to complete subordination by contrast, and are further subdued by neglect to make the most of the culminating scenes. Notwithstanding the regrettable omissions, and the weakness of the libretto, "Cavalleria Rusticana" has a firm hold upon popular appreciation, and will undoubtedly maintain its present prominent position in the modern repertory for a long while, if not permanently, as opera-loving people of all countries pay to it the homage of sincere praise.

The Rhinegold

AFTER THE ORIGINAL PAINTING BY H. HOLIDAY

THE RHINE MAIDENS: *The sleeping gold we do guard*
Carefully watch the slumberer's couch
Her food in it does the water boil.

THE NIBELUNGENLIED.

BY RICHARD WAGNER.

INTRODUCTORY THE RHINE GOLD.

IT WAS a work no less remarkable than it was stupendous that Wagner imposed upon himself when he set about the herculean task of rendering the myths of the Nibelunge Not into a composite and consistent drama for lyrical interpretation. The immediate inspiration which influenced him to such an effort was derived from Karl Simrock's epic poem celebrating the deeds of the German Dædalus, who by the aid of borrowed wings triumphed over his enemies in many astounding conflicts. But though the theme thus treated afforded a suggestion to Wagner, the legends, derived from the Eddas, and other northern sources, were related with such disregard for sequence and so abstract in motive, that to reduce them to the semblance of a drama it became necessary to carefully gather the disjointed and irrelevant incidents and combine them in harmonious agreement. The conception for lyric composition was not completed, however, by this consistent concentration, for the greater consideration remained, of giving to each character some distinctly human trait, and thus creating the good and evil, placing them in natural antagonism, so as not only to point a moral, but also to express Wagner's artistic ideas, both as poet and musician.

To accomplish his pretentious purpose years of preliminary preparation were necessary, which Wagner entered upon by a long and painstaking study of Norse mythology and those Teutonic legends associated with the Rhine. His first attempt to treat the tales dramatically was made in 1848, by writing a tragedy entitled "Death of Siegfried," which, however, was so incomplete, from his standpoint, that his original intention to set the work to music was abandoned. But pursuing the conception which had prompted his ambitious undertaking, in 1850 Wagner wrote a three-act drama, which he called "Wieland, the Smith," that followed in natural sequence the story of "Siegfried," but there were omissions noticeable to his artistic perceptions, which he set resolutely to supply by writing another three-act drama, "Young Siegfried." The production of this latter work emphasized to him the importance of introducing a more distinct motive than appeared in his previous efforts, in order that the Nibelungen myth might be reduced to an harmonious and consistent whole. It may be truly said the Tetralogy is an evolution from a concept that contained the smallest germ of his original purpose, for its stages of development are well defined. Thus we cannot fail to observe that the transpositions of his subjects were made to accommodate them to new ideas suggested by the minor dramas as he wrote them. It was in 1851 that Wagner decided to precede "Young Siegfried" with a preliminary drama which should tell the story of "The Rhine Gold," and follow this with a three-act tragedy devoted to the fortunes of Siegfried's parents, and to the expatriation of Brunhilde from Walhalla. By this decision the complete story was separated into what is really four dramas, but which taken as a whole compose a single tragedy, wherein the destinies of gods and men are indissolubly bound together.

Of the difficulties which beset Wagner in this work he wrote: "When I tried to dramatize the most important incidents of the Nibelungen myths in 'Siegfried's Death,' I found it imperative that I should indicate a number of antecedent

SIEGFRIED AND THE RHINE MAIDENS

facts, so as to bring the principal events into strong relief. But I was able only to *narrate* these subordinate matters, where I felt it imperative, for proper dramatic effects, that they should be embodied in the action. To resolve this difficulty I wrote 'Siegfried,' but my purpose was not fulfilled thereby, for the inconsistency still remained. In an effort to remove all objections I wrote 'The Valkyrie' and 'The Rhine Gold,' and thus contrived to incorporate all that was needful to make the action tell its own tale."

The complete poem was printed in 1853, and in the same year the score was begun as Wagner thus relates: "During a sleepless night I was spending at an inn in Spezzia, the music of 'The Rhine Gold' came to me. Straightway I returned home and set to work," which was finished the following year. In 1856 Wagner announced completion of the score for the "Valkyrie," and he at once set about the composition of "Siegfried," but pecuniary difficulties compelled him to turn his attention to other productions that promised immediate profit. It was thus he came to write "Tristan and Isolde." After an interruption of nearly ten years Wagner was able to resume composition of the score of "Siegfried" through assistance given him by Ludwig II., of Bavaria.

Retiring to Triebschen, his villa near Lucerne, in 1865 Wagner pursued his task, under most favorable influences, and completed the score of "Siegfried" and the "Gotterdammerung" by April, 1874, the initial performance of which took place at the Bayreuth theatre, built for the purpose, in August, 1876.

The "Nibelungen Ring" comprises four dramas, viz.: "The Rhine Gold," considered as an introductory to the tragedy proper, "The Valkyrie," "Siegfried," and "Gotterdammerung" (Twilight, or Fall of the Gods).

A precis of the trilogy, considering "The Rhine Gold" as a proem to the drama proper, may be given as follows: Wotan, who is the embodiment of ambition, is made the chief character, or hero, of the story, who though supreme deity in the mythology, longs for a power beyond that which he has obtained. In nature there is no type of perfectly satisfied desire, and so to invest his characters with finite, or comprehensible, attributes, Wagner represents Wotan as being opposed by two races of foes who continually threaten his supremacy. These enemies of the gods are giants and dwarfs, the latter being known in the legends as "Nibelungen," whence the title of the Cyclus is derived. The gods, giants, and dwarfs are all endowed with supernatural abilities, but, opposing each other, there is a limit set upon their respective powers to harm. Complete mastery may be obtained, however, by he who gains possession of the magic treasure, called the "Rhine Gold," which has many marvelous properties. So brilliant is this gold that it illumines, as a lamp, the caverns of the Rhine, and whoso makes from it a helmet may become invisible at will or assume any shape desired, while as a ring it becomes a talisman

HAGEN KILLS ORTLIEB IN THE PRESENCE OF THE QUEEN OF IRELAND.

of power. To obtain this wondrous treasure, Wotan employs all conceivable means, prostitutes his godly functions, endures many vicissitudes of fickle fortune, sacrifices his freedom, and when by these vain arts he finally succeeds, he falls before the curse that possession of gold entails. But though he steals the gold he cannot gain the ring, which remains in the hands of his enemies, and thus failing to possess the insignia of power, Wotan is overwhelmed with a dread that the downfall of the gods is at hand, unless, perchance, he shall have the help of some fearless and perfect being, who will secure this great treasure for him. After many futile efforts that ever plunge him into deeper despair, and which finally lead to Siegmund's death, Wotan abandons his mad desire and with bitterness of woe invites the fate which he sees approaching.

In the hour of his deepest despondency, when hope is gone, and he waits pronouncement of his doom, Wotan is roused from his dejection by a deliverer, by Siegfried, who is stranger to fear, but who is also offspring of guilt, whose parents have borne the punishment of death for their offence, that he might live. Siegfried, noble of aspect, fearless of soul, sinewy of limb, begets Wotan's admiration, who henceforth lives in the young hero's adventures. With solicitude and pride, Wotan watches Siegfried forge the sword invincible, exults over the death of the dragon, rejoices when Siegfried gains the ring, gives thanks when the poison cup is escaped, and Brunhilde is awakened. These triumphs save freed the world from the curse of gold, and thus finishing his godly labors Siegfried dies; but by overcoming the

THE RHINE GOLD

FUNERAL OF SIEGFRIED

evil ambitions of the world he has won Brunhilde, the daughter of Wotan, who, when the pyre is lighted upon which lies the body of her husband, Siegfried, she boldly submits herself to the consuming flames, declaring it is not gold, nor ring, nor splendor, but love alone that is all powerful. In the ancient Norse legend Kremhilde is a heroine that takes precedence of Brunhilde, who is represented as queen of Iceland, and it is she who resolves to avenge Siegfried's death. After a residence of thirteen years with her brother, Gunther, king of the Burgundians, she entertains proposal to become the wife of Attila, king of the Huns. Thirteen years later Gunther, and Hagen, who has committed many crimes meantime, accompanied by a host of their followers, are invited by Rudiger to the court of Attila, but on their arrival all are slaughtered save Gunther and Hagen, who are made captives and taken before Attila and Kremhilde. Hagen has gained possession of the magic ring and brought it to Worms, where fearing its power to work evil he has buried it in the Rhine. Kremhilde commands him to produce the ring or reveal where it is hidden, but he answers by declaring his purpose to keep its resting place secret so long as the king, Gunther, lives. Directly the head of Gunther is shown him as a proof of death, but Hagen still refuses, whereupon Kremhilde snatches the sword which Hagen has used since Siegfried's death and strikes off his hated head. Her savage act horrifies the whole assemblage and is resented by Hildebrand, a Hunnish warrior, who drives his sword through her body and she falls dead before Attila.

The story of "The Rhine Gold," as treated by Wagner in his dramatic poem, is one of exquisite charm and conveys an excellent moral under an investiture of sublime though weird imagination. The opening scene is marvelously beautiful, showing three lovely nymphs, known as Wellgunda, Woglinda, and Flosshilda, disporting in translucent waters, in and out, through rock caverns of the deep. These witching sea-maids are daughters of the Rhine god, to whom is committed the guardianship of the "Rhine Gold," which may be seen diffusing a mellow light from its bed upon a peak about which the nymphs are at play. While thus pursuing their pleasures in the waters, the sea-maid sisters are approached by Alberich, a Nibelungen, or dwarf, who with his race lives in caverns of the earth, where they are metal workers. Really, these are spirits of darkness who seldom see the light of day, and their forms are misshapen as becomes such as are doomed to existence in eternal gloom.

Alberich stealthily gropes his way to a point where he can plainly see the nymphs and hear their conversation, and there he pauses to listen. The sisters admonish each other of their sacred charge, and pledge their care to guard the treasure which their father, entrusting, warned them would be sought by a cunning dwarf who is foe of gods and men. They have no fear, however, for to them it has been made known that none shall seize the "Rhine Gold" who has not purged his heart of love. When Alberich has watched the nymphs for a while their grace and beauty so fascinate him that he boldly pursues them, but they dart hither and thither, always eluding his grasp and teasingly beckon him to continue the chase, until his patience is exhausted. When, tired by the vain pursuit, Alberich would rest, mortified by his disappointment, suddenly the opalescent waters glow with light from the "Rhine Gold" treasure, and the nymphs hail it with song that expose its marvelous virtues.

Astonished by the sight, the sulphurous, hairy, swarthy dwarf eagerly inquires what precious thing is this, which with its golden gleams and passionate glow lights like moon and stars these liquid caves of perpetual night, to which Wellgunda answering tells him:

"The realm of the world
By him shall be won,
Who a ring from the Rhine Gold
Shall fashion and don."

THE RHINE GOLD.

This magic property of the treasure, as well also its phosphorescent glow, excites Alberich's cupidity and curiosity to examine it more closely and to ascertain its value, but Flosshilda admonishes that:

> "Our father he hath strictly charged us
> To safely guard for him the brilliant ore,
> That no secret foe may from the flood
> Steal the treasure and compass his woe."

Such admonition it were well to heed. Woglinda confesses, but she fears no loss of the wondrous gold, reminding her solicitous sisters that it has ever been known no one may hope to gain the precious trove

> "Who by the power of love has been unmoved;
> And least of all the lecherous gnome,
> Who hath no soul save lustful fire
> Like sulphurous surge of a seething sea."

When Alberich thus discovers from the nymphs the secret power that resides within the golden nugget, and how by renunciation of love he may possess it, he soliloquizes:

> "The wealth of the world I must win,
> If the boon of love be denied me.
> Mock as you may, my cunning shall match you,
> The Nibelung's purpose to gain,
> To fashion the ring of revenge
> All love I freely forswear."

Having thus spoken, the impassioned dwarf wrenches the gold from the peak and bearing it in triumph he plunges towards the bowels of the earth, the three nymphs pursuing and screaming, "Help! Woe!" as darkness supervenes to hide the scene.

In the next scene light dawns gradually, until there is revealed lofty heights which represent the abode of the gods. As the sun rises, its rays fall in splendor upon the golden turrets of a lordly castle that crowns a mountain peak, and on the flowery slopes are Wotan and his consort, Fricka, the chief deities of northern mythology. As they slowly awaken from their slumbers, they look with satisfaction upon the palace that has been reared in a night for their abode by the hands of giants. Fricka's pride is soon changed to grief, however, as she remembers that Fafner and Fasolt, the giant builders, have been promised the sun, moon, and the fair Freia, as a reward for their labors. Freia is Fricka's sister, goddess of youth and beauty, and guardian of the sacred apples, from the eating of which the gods derive their youth and strength. Fricka is dismayed by the thought of losing her sister, and bitterly bewails the fatal promise, which she would avert by violating the compact were it not inscribed upon Wotan's spear; but she turns upon her husband with such condemning words that he regrets his rashness and seeks a means whereby he may escape the impending results of his agreement.

There is only one to whom he may apply for aid in this dire extremity, Loki, the god of fire, famous for his trickery and daring, so Wotan makes haste to summon this powerful deity. While waiting Loki's coming, Freia rushes upon the stage, terrified and distracted, and in impassioned speech beseeches Wotan to save her from the two giants who are in hot pursuit. Thor and Froh, her brothers, are also implored to give their protection, and these stand disputing with the giants when Loki appears, to whom appeal is made to concert some means whereby to cancel the bargain. In reply Loki tells Wotan that he has sought diligently throughout the world for something that is more precious than youth and love, for such a gain would be esteemed beyond all other desires, but his quest has been vain. Even giants might freely exchange all their possessions for such a treasure, but where may it be found? Loki then proceeds to tell them of his search, and to philosophize upon the vanities of the world, the ties that bind the hearts of gods as well as of men. Knowing what the giants will demand, a rigid compliance with Wotan's agreements, which means the sacrifice of Freia, he describes his wanderings through the world's wide wastes seeking a ransom, but has learned that there is not enough of wealth that men would exchange for woman's worth. He had asked of whatever there is of

THE RHINE GOLD

life in water, earth and air, where strength is manifest and buds burst into blossom, but found none that were willing to match woman's love and worth with mortal possessions; that would barter love for lucre. And yet his search has not been wholly vain, for a creature sinister has he found who hath love eschewed, which Loki thus explains:

> "One only did I find who
> Forswearing love did seek his further aims;
> One who did sneer at woman's love,
> A cursèd gift to seize
> Alberich, the dwarf sinister
> Who by his strength has raped the gold
> From nymphs whom Wotan set on watch
> To guard it in the Rhine's flood
> This foul Nibelung doth hold it now,
> As higher than all woman's worth.
> Against the wails of woeful maids
> Who cry and pine for its recovery.
> These maids have my promised help
> And Loki must his pledge redeem"

Fasolt and Fafner listen attentively to Loki's tale of wanderings, and with curiosity aroused they ask what marvel is mixed with the "Rhine Gold" that Alberich esteems it so vastly. "Oh, it is only a bauble!" answers Loki, "a thing to please a child's eye, but yet it conceals a wondrous power, for if by skillful hands a ring be wrought of this glowing nugget, the wearer may have a measureless might to gain not only wealth but mastery of the world."

Fricka urges her husband to seek this magic gold to win, which he expresses desire to do, and asks of Loki how if once obtained he may learn to fashion the treasure, which answering Loki thus replies:

> "It is only by runic magic
> That a ring from the gold may be wrought,
> And only he can form it
> Who the joy of love abjures
> And now, alas! it is too late.
> For Alberich through such abjuration,
> Hath already, by magic might,
> Rightly forged the mystic ring."

Excitedly, Thor exclaims: "Then mastered by the dwarf we soon must be, unless the ring be wrested from him! But how may this be done without renouncing love?"

"Quite easily," answers Loki; "what one thief has robbed may be stolen from him by another, and so let us rob the rogue, since duty 'tis to heed the appeals of the Rhine maidens and ease their grief by restoring to them the golden treasure."

Fafner's covetous cravings have grown beyond control by Loki's story of the marvelous power of the ring, and conceiving a purpose to barter his claims upon the goddess Freia for its possession, thus proposes:

> "Do you, Wotan, esteem Freia's worth
> As above the price of this glittering gold?
> Hear, Wotan, and be thou wise to listen —
> Freia we will leave to her freedom
> Since a way we found for the forfeit
> By which the Nibelung's gold may serve to
> Weary work was it building your palace,
> And fighter will it be to bind the dwarf
> Let Freia remain to us a pledge
> Until this Rhine Gold be paid for her lease."

Since the "Rhine Gold" has been in the keep of Alberich he has wrought a ring from it and by the power thus gained he has amassed immeasurable wealth and become supreme

"Heia oh! Heia oh! Hoio! Wau!"

over all his race of the under world. When the giants are informed of the power that follows possession of this marvelous treasure, they offer to release Wotan from his promise, upon condition that the "Rhine Gold" is delivered to them before nightfall, but they refuse to relinquish their rights under the compact until this is done, and despite her shrieks they carry Freia away to hold her as a hostage for performance of Wotan's agreement to produce the treasure. As the giants disappear with their captive, the gods, having lost the guardian of the golden apples, grow visibly old, and decrepit, which change in his beloved wife causes Wotan to quickly resolve to secure the mystic ring at whatever sacrifice; so bidding Loki direct the way, the two descend to the dark regions of the Nibelungen, through a cleft rock from which rises a cloud that gradually obscures from view the departing figures.

KRIEMHILDE KILLS HAGEN, BUT IS HERSELF SLAIN BY HILDEBRAND.

The opening of Scene III represents the home of the Nibelungs, a dank cavern ranging beyond the power of eye to fellow in the darkening shades, and cross tunnels extending in many directions. Alberich enters dragging Mime, his brother, by the ear, berating him with severe words, and promising him the lash if he does not work faster. Mime, all a-tremble, from fear of punishment, has been put to the task of making a helmet from the "Rhine Gold," a "tarnhelm" as it is called, which, if properly fashioned, gives to the wearer power to be transformed at will into the form of any creature, or to become invisible by wish. Alberich presently discovers that the magic cap is finished, for in his agitation Mime has let it fall to the ground, fearing to show it lest the workmanship be imperfect. Quickly Alberich seizes and places the helmet on his head, and finding it to be perfectly tries its property by wishing to dissolve. Instantly his form vanishes, a column of mist appearing where he stood, out of which his voice is heard reviling Mime, and when the latter expresses astonishment, a lash, heard and felt though unseen, serves to remind him that though invisible Alberich still has power to punish.

Groaning with pain Mime rolls upon the ground as Loki and Wotan descend to the cavern. Finding him writhing in agony from his hurts they ask the wretched dwarf the cause of his misery, that they may succor him. Mime bids them begone, for help no one can give since every behest of his brutish brother he must obey, being bound in slavish bondage. "Bondage!" Loki exclaims, "by what might hath Mime become so reduced?" Whereat the dwarf fully explains, that Alberich has secured the "Rhine Gold" from which by evil arts he has forged a wondrous ring that hath given him mastery over all the Nibelung race, whom he forces now to endless labor, digging treasure from the earth to smelt and beat, and heap it in a mighty hoard whereby to win the world. That more than treasure of gold has Alberich gained, for through slavish labor he has now a helmet, as wondrous as the ring, which by magic trick doth make him changeable at will, to form of any living thing, or to vanish at his wish.

As the three are thus discoursing Alberich appears, driving before him a host of dwarfs bearing loads of gold and silver handiwork, which is laid in a pile. Perceiving Wotan and Loki he lays the lash upon Mime for speaking with strangers, and drawing the ring from his finger he holds it a menace towards his Nibelung slaves, who, with howls, escape into dark passages of the cavern. Alberich now advances towards Wotan and Loki and demands to know the object of

"WOTAN HUNTED! ANSWER."

THE RHINE GOLD.

their visit, at which Loki answers that it is to learn the truth of many wonderful stories which are being told of his wealth and power. Alberich, through magic wit, recognizes his guests and perceives their purpose, but feels so secure in his puissance as wearer of the ring and helmet, and master of the treasures of the earth, that he defies the gods and threatens to bind them as his slaves; that as he has himself forsworn the sweets of love, so all who live shall also abjure it:

> "Ye wantons, I charge ye beware,
> Full soon all must submit
> To the power of my masterful might;
> And your winsomest women
> I shall make slaves to a dwarf's delights."

Wotan is so angered by these foul boasts that he threatens to strike the wanton wretch, but is restrained by Loki, who steps between, having a mind to trick the dwarf by flattery. With such purpose in view he tells Alberich he must not be surprised that people marvel at the power which he is said to possess; that one so mighty, who by his wish may heap up riches beyond all the dreams of fancy, may well claim homage from the sun and starry hosts. But even more wonderful is the tale that all the Nibelung multitude, whose service yields such countless treasure, and that masterful Mime, who such wondrous talisman has wrought, doth servilely obey his will, counting his power greater than skill or cunning, since 'tis they who by magic might have forged the ring and fashioned the mystic tarnhelm. With such adulation does Loki please the listening ear of Alberich, but with hope to expose his secret, Loki falls to questioning the dwarf as to the probable permanence of his powers, shrewdly asking:

> "If while you sleep
> Some thief the ring should ravish,
> How may you keep
> The treasure now you cherish?"

With a sneer of contempt, Alberich answers that Loki being fool himself imagines others to be equally witless, but to relieve his ignorance he tells the god of fire that he is guarded no more by the magic ring than by the tarnhelm (helmet) which has been shaped with such cunning skill by Mime, prince of artful smiths, that placed upon his head it gives him power to change his shape to any creature, or to become invisible at will. "With such protection against thieves and treachery, I am perfectly shielded, thou pious but fraudulent friend!"

Loki takes no offence at the dwarf's imputations, whose mightiness he acknowledges, but whose amazing power he asks may be exhibited, saying:

> "Wonders such as these immortals never saw;
> Prodigious mind, to master nature's law.
> Such to perform is proof external
> That power is thine to live eternal."

"Thinkest thou I lie!" thunders the boastful and indignant dwarf. "Thy doubt shall quickly be dispelled." So saying, Alberich puts on the magic tarnhelm, whereupon he is instantly changed into a serpent of monstrous size and appalling aspect. Loki and Wotan simulate intense fear at such terrifying creature, but when Alberich resumes his former shape the crafty gods profess that a greater wonder it would be to see him become a toad! "Bah!" shouts the dwarf, "nothing is easier." And again placing the helmet on his head he mutters a mystic formula, when,

THE RHINE GOLD.

behold Alberich disappears, and where he stood there creeps a toad!

The opportunity which Loki and Wotan have sought has been gained through the cunning of the fire god, who now commands Wotan to seize the reptile with firm grip, while he tears the tarnhelm from the creature's head, thus rendering him powerless. The dwarf resumes his human shape under the foot of Wotan and amid his shrieks and curses the gods bind him strongly and drag him away captive, mounting upward whence they came.

In the fourth and last scene, the entrance to Walhalla, abode of the gods, is again represented, veiled in a gray mist. Loki and Wotan come upon the stage dragging the dwarf after them, who is cursing and threatening his enemies, but they disregard his ravings and remind him that in secure captivity he has no power to harm; but advise if he would seek vengeance to first obtain by ransom his release. Realizing his helpless condition, Alberich asks what ransom they would demand, and is told that no less the prize must be than all his heaped up gold. Alberich denounces them as a robbing and ravenous race, but to himself consoles

> "If I retain for myself the ring,
> I may give the hoard without grief;
> For by the marvel of the gem
> I may regain the treasure store
> And wreak my vengeance still."

Consenting to yield up the heap of gold, one hand is first released and Alberich kisses the ring while murmuring his commands summoning the Nibelungs to bring up the treasure hoard. Obedient to the call, the dwarfs come out of their burrows in the earth bearing trays of jewels which they deposit in a pile before the gods. Alberich begs that the tarnhelm may be spared him, but Loki insists that it be cast with the rest, whereupon with direst maledictions the envenomed dwarf exclaims:

> "Thou thief accursed, thy crime shall yet atone.
> He who made the cap may yet another loan,
> By might of which my wrongs shall be redressed
> And thou enslaved, my power shall be confessed
> The hoard is yours, nought now remains.
> Your promise keep, loose thou my chains."

The wily dwarf fancies he may escape by sacrificing his hoard and the magic helmet, but Wotan discovers the ring, and this too he demands. Alberich gnashes his teeth with anger and swears the ring he will not surrender, since to him it is as dear as life:

> "Such murderous deceit, conceived in deadly malice!
> Thou shamefully doth charge me with a crime thyself wouldst commit!
> Truly ye would have ravished the gold from its guardians.
> Hadst thou the skill to forge the ring my cunning made
> He is thrice a thief who steals the craftsman's product,
> And for his gain there shall rise a brood of curses!"

But his cries of rage and his piteous pleadings are without avail, for, impatient of the dwarf's petitions, Wotan tears it from his finger and holding it aloft triumphantly felicitates his good fortune. Alberich is now released, and rising from the ground, laughs demoniacally and before disappearing pronounces a curse upon all who keep the ring:

> "Hold thou the ring close to thy heart,
> But my curses thereon thou canst never escape."

THE RHINE GOLD.

As Loki and Wotan are contemplating with pleasure the vast hoard of gold, Froh, Thor and Fricka enter, who inquire as to the result; of the god's adventure, upon which Loki points to the glittering pile:

"By force and by cunning we have obtained
This hoard that may our Freia ransom"

At the same moment the two giants, Fafner and Fasolt, come upon the scene leading the fair but sorrowing Freia between them, whom the gods welcome joyfully; but she is restrained by the giants, who demand the ransom, which though appearing large, must be in quantity great enough to pile about and cover her entirely from view. The giants now fix their staves in the ground to represent the height and width of Freia's form, about which Loki and Froh heap up the treasure, packing the pieces closely together, while Fricka and Wotan rave at the disgrace of having to buy the goddess' freedom. Thor and Loki continue to pile the treasure about the winsome woman until she appears to be quite hidden, but Fafner measuring carefully with his eye, discovers a hair struggling through a crevice of the heap and fiercely demands that something more be added. But the hoard has all been used, all save the helmet and the ring which Wotan longs to save. To hide the fluttering tress of hair the tarnhelm is sacrificed, when lo! Fasolt, by covetous scrutiny, spies through the golden envelope a glow from Freia's eye, and this he insists shall be closed by other treasure. Seeing the ring on Wotan's finger the giants declare it shall be added to the store, to stop the chink, but Wotan persists that all the world may not wrest the ring from his hand, whereat Fasolt pulls Freia away pronouncing that she is forfeit forever. She cries for help, and Fricka, Froh and Thor beseech the god to save her, but Wotan remains immovable. Suddenly the stage darkens, and from a cleft in the rock there issues an opaline glare that reveals Erda, the all-wise, rising partly out of the ground. Stretching out her hand towards Wotan she warns him to flee the curse of the ring:

"Three daughters, Norns of fate,
Were born to me ere the world began;
By these was I called to counsel thee
That direst danger day of gloom
Dawns for all the gods;
Hence I warn thee, beware the ring!"

Wotan beseeches Erda to give him information that may help him avert her sinister foreboding, but she refuses to speak further, and disappears, leaving him to ponder her words. After some reflection Wotan casts the ring upon the treasure heap and the giants accept the prize. Freia is released and returns to the gods, who immediately recover their youth and vigor, which is celebrated with great rejoicing. The two giants now possess the mystic treasure, but the curse which Alberich laid upon it at once appears. Fafner produces a sack in which he proceeds to place all the gold, but Fasolt disputes his right to the whole possession and calls the gods to divide the hoard equally. The crafty Loki anticipating the result that must follow, advises Fasolt to leave the gold for possession of the ring, which counsel he adopts; but the curse of the ring is always upon the one who keeps it, so the moment Fasolt seizes the fatal gift, he is driven to kill Fafner, and after committing this crime he carries off the whole of the treasure.

THE RHINE GOLD.

Wotan, in whom there resides many of the virtues that glorify mankind, horror-stricken by the consequences of the golden curse, as well as melancholy over the threatened doom of the gods, announces his intent to descend to the abode of Erda to consult her how he may avert the prophecy she has made, and lay the evil spell that oppresses him. Fricka compassionates Wotan's depression, and to restore his happiness reminds him of the castle the giants erected, of Walhalla (heaven), to which splendors she now calls his attention and reminds him that this blissful place is established for their mutual enjoyment. At this Thor, the god of thunder, and Froh, the god of light, ascend into the clouds above, where they conjure a storm; peals of fierce thunder are heard, and flashes of lightning illumine, with blinding glare, the clouds and mountain peaks; the storm quickly spends its force, however, and there succeeds a burst of radiance, and a glittering rainbow of quivering hues is seen bridging the space between the valley and Walhalla, home of the gods. Wotan is fascinated by the glorious prospect and invites the gods and goddesses to follow him to the heavenly city. As he steps upon the irradiant arch a wail rises from the Rhine daughters who lament the loss of their treasure and entreat the gods to restore it. The answer returned is accompanied by mocking laugh as Loki utters:

"Ye water nymphs, why weep ye in our hearing?
Hear what Wotan hath devised for your pleasure.
If no longer in the brightness of the gold ye may rejoice,
There remains for you still the splendor in which the gods now enter."

To this the nymphs, still wailing, make their reply, pointing the moral of lustful ambitions:

"Truth and faith can be found only in the depths;
Falsehood and cowardice alone can suit themselves in the glories on high."

As these words are uttered the nymphs sink into deeps of the Rhine, mourning for their lost treasure, while the gods move, a celestial procession, across the rainbow archway that connects the earth with Walhalla. The scene is a beautiful one, and withal sublime and impressive, a fitting conclusion to the overture to the tragedies that succeed in the trilogy.

Valkyrie

(AFTER THE ORIGINAL PAINTING BY K. DIELITZ)

WOTAN— "Farewell, my brave and beautiful child!
. . . .
Thy bed shall be lit by torches more brilliant
Than ever for bridal have burned;
Fiery gleams shall girdle the fell
With terrible searchings."

ACT III. SCENE III

THE VALKYRIE.

AGNER'S great trilogy, often referred to as the Cyclus, properly begins with the legend of the "Valkyrie," a story of extraordinary interest and which in its entirety conveys a lesson of moral worth that adds infinitely to its charm, notwithstanding some of the situations are compromising. In the "Rhinegold" Introduction we find the motive of the drama, but the fortunes of the gods are followed consistently in the "Valkyrie." Wotan gained Walhalla, but dwelling amid all possible blessings did not repress his longing for greater power, or mitigate his gloom over Erda's prophecy. His desire to repossess the magic ring grows until not even the love of Fricka can restrain his purpose longer, so with resolute intent he assumes a disguise and passing into the underworld finds and woos the earth goddess whose wisdom enables her to read the past, know the present, and tell the future. Wotan so passionately professes his loving devotion that Erda is beguiled, and she bears him eight daughters, who are to become his mighty assistants in the strife which she had foretold. The gods are so far outnumbered by mortals that Wotan resolves to recruit his strength from among the strong races that have come into existence, to which end accordingly the fiercest warriors are invited to his abode. But in order that men may be hardened and trained for fighting, war must be encouraged, and so Wotan waves his spear over the earth, by which strife is engendered among nations, and battles are waged everywhere. His eight daughters, called Valkyries, signifying *the choosers*, are commanded to ride over the earth each day and on flying steeds bear away to Walhalla the bravest of the slain. These warriors are revived the moment they reach the celestial hall, where they sit at a festal board eating boars' heads, and regaling themselves with mead, drunk out of the skulls of their enemies. For exercise and training, these translated warriors spend their days also in fighting each other, but every wound inflicted in such combats upon the heavenly fields is immediately cured by magic balm, and death can come no more.

Wotan powerfully protects Walhalla by recruiting his forces from the bravest that fall in the strifes of the world, but great as is his spiritual army, he cannot dismiss the fears excited by Erda's prophecy. He longs to recover the ring that Fafner still possesses, for should it fall into the hands of Alberich, the ireful dwarf will not fail to revenge himself upon the gods. Wotan is bound by his promises, however, and by the laws of heaven he cannot himself forcibly recover a gift which he has once bestowed. To accomplish his purpose without violating any canon of the gods, Wotan resolves to beget a son who shall be his unconscious emissary, to oppose the offspring which Erda has predicted Alberich will raise up to avenge the rape of the ring, and who will aid him to gain the coveted talisman. He accordingly disguises himself as a mortal, taking the name of Wolsung (which signifies a mighty lord), and becomes a habitant of the earth, where he marries a woman who bears him twin children, son and daughter, which are named respectively Siegmund and Sieglinda. While these are still young, but in the absence of Siegmund and Wolsung (Wotan), Hunding, chief of the Niedings, a maliciously cruel hunter, finds their hut in the forest, which he burns to the ground, and when Wolsung's mortal wife attempts to escape he slays her and carries off Sieglinda. When Wolsung and his son, Siegmund, return they find their home in ashes, and contemplate the crime of Hunding with feelings of vengeance, which they make a vow to glut upon their foes; but neither finds opportunity to punish their enemy, until after Siegmund has grown to manhood, when his father suddenly disappears, leaving nothing behind save a wolfskin coat which the young man puts on and enters into the strifes and adventures which fate has destined him to encounter. In the meantime, Hunding has kept Sieglinda a captive in his forest

A VALKYRIE BATTLE MAIDEN

THE VALKYRIE

home, which he has strongly built around the trunk of a mighty ash tree, and when she is grown to womanhood he makes her his wife against her will, and prepares a great feast to celebrate the nuptials. Wotan, in disguise, attends the wedding, which he makes no effort to prevent, but drawing his sword he plunges it so deeply into the heart of the ash tree that only the hilt remains in view, and promises that the weapon shall be his who has the strength to withdraw it. To Sieglinda, however, he confides the secret that her lost brother, Siegmund, will one day gain possession of the weapon, and that his identity will be made known to her by his power to obtain it.

The opening scene of the "Valkyrie" presents a view of Hunding's dwelling, through the centre of which grows a great tree with wide extending branches shading and protecting the roof. A low fire is blazing upon the hearth of the large hall, but no one is visible. A terrible storm is raging without, making the night hideous, when Siegmund, who has lost his way, and is quite exhausted, fleeing from his enemies, appears at the door seeking refuge, but pauses a moment awaiting invitation to enter. Seeing no one he steps inside, and staggers to the hearth, where he throws himself upon a bear's skin, uttering, "Whose house this may be, yet here I must rest." A moment later Sieglinda enters from another room, believing it is her husband who has returned. Discovering that the person is a stranger, she advances and accosts him, but Siegmund is too tired to answer. She draws closer, and thinking the visitor sick or dead, she bends above him to listen if his heart is beating. At this Siegmund lifts his head a little and faintly asks for water. Moved by compassion Sieglinda quickly fills a drinking horn and offers it to his parched lips, when with thankful heart he asks, "Who is't restores me to life?" For reply Sieglinda tells him she is wife of Hunding, who will give him a guestful greeting if he will tarry till he come. Siegmund is confounded to thus learn that he is in the house of his relentless enemy, and without weapon to make his defence, for he has been at war, and being pressed by numbers has shivered his spear and shield, counting it good fortune to have escaped without many wounds. With show of great kindness Sieglinda fills a horn with mead, tasting it first, at his request, and

KRIEMHILDA DISCOVERS THE BODY OF HER LOVER

gives him to drink, whereat he shows emotion, perceiving that which moves his heart to love: a woman charitable of mind, discreet of speech, and beautiful of person. After drinking he would depart, fearful that his presence may bring ill-hap to the house, but she by gentle persuasion induces him to remain.

As the two stand in silence gazing upon one another, Hunding suddenly enters fully armed, and by stern look would seem to ask the stranger's purpose, which Sieglinda is quick to explain, whereupon Hunding gives Siegmund welcome, and orders that supper be prepared. While this is being done, Hunding closely scrutinizes Siegmund, observing with astonishment the likeness of his features to those of Sieglinda, but conceals his surprise, and questions his guest as to the misfortune that has brought him hither. To these inquiries Siegmund relates the mournful tale of his wanderings and sorrows:

"Wolfung, the mighty, was my father!
As twins came we into the world,
My sister Sieglinda and I.
But sister, mother, quickly I lost,
A parent dear, and a playmate fair,
Powerful and brave was my sire
But foes he numbered many.
Youthful was I, yet with him I wandered
Through forests dense in quest of prey
Alas, once when we from the hunt returned,
We found our hut in ashes laid,
Its timbers smouldering from a fiery blast,
Beside the heap my slaughtered mother lay,
But of my sister no trace was found.
With me my father fled his wrath to cherish;
Thus in the forest has my life been spent."

Death to the Burgundians !"

THE VALKYRIE.

Hunding interrupts to confess that he has heard of this warrior pair, who relate such fearsome stories, but a Wolsung he has not known till now. Sieglinda's interest is so excited that she craves to learn more, to know the fortunes of his father, and at her urging Siegmund continues:

"My father pursuing a host of Niedings fell upon us.
But so many were made victims of our might
That, fleeing, the rest sought safety in retreat
Like the wind we chased them without mercy!
By chance I separated from my father
I wearily sought but could not find him.
Thus left alone was I, with only a wolf's skin.
After this shunned I the woods.
And sheltered with heroes and women.
But far and near, where'er I searched,
If for friend, or maid to love, I found not.
Nothing could I win, for ill luck was mine
When doing what was right, I did wrong to others,
And that which I thought ill, others holy contended for ;
So that I was ever involved in feud,
And strife came wherever I strayed
Did I seek pleasure, pain was my portion.
Thus then am I called 'Woeful' rightly,
For, unwillingly, woe I must work."

By this confession of Siegmund's unhappy fortunes, and his boasted valor in contending with the Niedings, Hunding discovers him to be an enemy, and begrudges the hospitality he has extended. But Sieglinda is fascinated by the stranger, and, lured by his tale of hapless ventures, beseeches that he tell in what attack his weapons were last used. Siegmund, thereupon, with much vigor, relates how in defence of a maiden whom a chiding kin would compel to marry a churl she did not love, he fought single-handed against countless foes until his weapons were broken and the maiden slain at his feet.

By this dire tale Sieglinda is deeply moved, accounting it so true of her own experiences, but Hunding is inflamed with anger, and rising from his seat he fiercely denounces Siegmund as an enemy who flying from a just vengeance would seek refuge at the hearth of his foe ; the laws of hospitality shall give him protection for the night, but on the morrow at dawn of day Hunding challenges him to combat, and with lowering looks would seem to threaten immediate attack. Sieglinda interposes between the men, at which Hunding harshly orders her to leave the hall, and preparing his evening draught wait him in another room. Painfully she moves towards the pantry, where she fills a drinking horn, casting betimes furtive looks at Siegmund, and then by eloquent earnestness fixes her gaze upon a particular spot in the ash tree. Hunding, with show of great impatience, commands her again to leave the room, and as she passes out he takes his weapons from the tree, to which he proudfully points,

THE VALKYRIE.

bidding Siegmund to beware on the morrow, since hospitality may protect him no longer than the night. Siegmund makes no reply to the vainglorious hunter, who, casting a contemptuous look, retires sullenly to his chamber and noisily bolts the door after him.

Scene III.—Siegmund, now left alone, reclines upon a couch and reflects upon his weaponless condition, by which he may fall a victim to a treacherous foe. Suddenly he calls to mind a promise which his father has made, to provide the sword Nothung when dire extremity should come upon him, and rousing out of his dejection he cries, "Wolsung! Wolsung! Where is the sword?" In answer to his appeal, the fire upon the hearth blazes brightly and the light therefrom reveals a sword-hilt, plainly visible, protruding from the tree-trunk. Siegmund hails the gladsome sight with exultation, and as the powerfully moving sword melody is sounded, he sings of his love for Sieglinda, whom he resolves to rescue whatever be the hazard.

As the last notes of the singer expire the fire becomes extinguished and darkness supervenes, while a death-like stillness settles on the scene. The quiet is at length disturbed by Sieglinda, who, robed in white, steals softly into the room to apprise Siegmund of his danger. In quick but whispered speech she tells him how she has mingled a drug in Hunding's drink that will hold him fast in the embrace of sleep to give time for hasty escape, and bids the stranger flee. Siegmund ardently interrupts to ask what cause has she for fear, whereupon Sieglinda relates in impassioned song the story of the good sword Nothung, that while the guests were making merry celebrating the wedding of Hunding with maid whom ne'er he wooed, and whose misery he entailed, there entered a guest unbidden, a man with one eye darkened, whose looks so fierce that others shrank with awe, but smiled he upon her as he unslung his sword and with arm all powerful thrust it heart-deep into the ash tree trunk, saying, "To none shall the prize be fated, but who can pluck it forth." Thereafter hundreds of warriors, stout and valiant, have striven to loose the weapon from its binding sheath, though none succeeded. But secret to others, it is no mystery to her, for she has divined the hero who thus planted the sword, and knows the name of that one for whom it is withheld. Thus, with anguish of desire, she cries out:

"If in my need such friend could find,
Help and love might yet be mine."

The cry reaches Siegmund's heart, who by this tale of wonder has discovered to him his long-lost sister, and fervidly embracing her declares he is that friend who weapon and wife doth claim: that her sufferings have been his own; and that to him has at last been given the power to avenge her woes. While thus expressing their glad surprise, the great entrance door of the hut is flung open by unseen hands, and through the way the full moon throws a flood of mellow light, which falling upon the pair covers them with a tide of splendor. The storm has passed, and a glorious spring night robes the landscape, which inspiring to tender passion, Siegmund draws Sieglinda to a bench, and seated thereon he sings:

"Winter's blasts have fled before the beauteous moon,
In mild ascendency now beams the coming spring." etc

To which the enraptured Sieglinda makes response that manifests her love, her trustfulness and her dependence:

"Thou art my joyous spring;
For thee my heart has fretted long,
Frost-fettered by repinings." etc.

Which many competent admirers of Wagner pronounce the loveliest melody, wrought in sweetest sentiment, that he ever composed. The passionate interview results in mutual recognition, by which their relations of brother and sister become known, and that of lover and mistress is established.

The sword, Sieglinda declares, was struck in the ash tree for him, whereupon, with exultant cry he seizes the exposed hilt, and with mighty effort plucks it from its fastness, and as she throws herself upon his breast he exclaims:

"Sister and bride be to me, thy brother.
Thereby to cherish the Wolsung name."

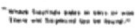

consummating an unnatural union which, for one of its results, shall bring forth Siegfried, the hero of the trilogy. The curtain falls on Act I as Siegmund

THE VALKYRIE

prompted by his passion to rescue Sieglinda from the cruel Hunding, bears her away a willing captive into the forest depths, where brother and sister become at once husband and wife

Act II.—The opening scene of Act II shows a wild and rocky pass in the mountains of the gods, exposing to view Wotan, who, armed with spear and shield, is conversing with Brunhilde, his daughter, chief of the eight Valkyries, who also appears clothed in armor. He informs her of the combat which will soon occur between Siegmund and Hunding, and bids her make ready her steed to descend to the earth to give Siegmund the victory.

Prompt to execute the commands of her father, Brunhilde starts upon her mission shouting the weird Valkyrie cry, "Ho-yo-to-ho." Making her way to a lofty peak, Brunhilde pauses, and looking back shouts to Wotan:

> "Listen, and behold, father! Trouble threateneth!
> The wrathful Fricka approacheth in her ram-drawn car."

The moment Brunhilde disappears Fricka arrives before the startled Wotan and a stormy scene ensues, wherein Fricka, as goddess of marriage, violently condemns her husband for having forsaken her to woo the goddess Erda, and for wedding a mortal maid. Thus angrily assailing him for infidelity she reprobates the incestuous union of Siegmund and Sieglinda, and by passionate remonstrance induces Wotan to revoke his decree and give the victory to Hunding, the dishonored husband. As this promise is given, Brunhilde's voice is heard in exultant song, and she is soon seen leading her horse, down a mountain path, which she hides in a cave and then approaches Fricka, who tells her Wotan awaits her with a new command, whereupon she drives away in her gilded chariot drawn by rams.

In Scene II Wotan is observed, in deep dejection, leaning against a rock, absorbed in gloomy foreboding, when Brunhilde advances, asking:

> "Father, what must thy child fulfil thee?
> Sad and downcast thou seemest!"

In measures of intense grief Wotan tells Brunhilde of the power exerted by Fricka, which has made him less free than the earth-born, and thereupon relates how he has been beguiled by Loki, and by his own ambitions, thirsting for possession of the fatal ring, which it had been his purpose should be recovered by Siegmund, even though warned by Erda of the evil fate that must befall his efforts; and he confesses to her his union with Erda, by which she, with eight sisters, were begotten, a war-maid band who shall gather souls of heroes slain in battle,

> "That an army of fearless heroes
> May guard me safe in Walhalla's hall."

But now, alas, that Siegmund is doomed, never shall he be freed from the curse of the ravished gold; never shall its bane be ended until Walhalla itself shall be destroyed, the gods annihilated and the end of all things be accomplished through the revengeful Alberich. Despairingly, but bitterly, to her inquiry, "Father, what shall I perform?" he answers:

> "Be thou a champion of Fricka;
> Guard then well her virgin vows;
> What e'er she wills, that also I confirm,
> For boundless now is my volition."

Brunhilde, distracted by her father's words, implores him to retract, and for the love he bears Siegmund, his son, permit that she protect him, but his promise to Fricka is inexorable, and impatiently he commands that she shall to Hunding give the victory. Horrified at such a purpose she utters a protest, at which Wotan frowns his indignation, and repeating his command disappears into the mountains, leaving Brunhilde terrified and bewildered. Fricka's jealous vengeance she is about to gratify; Wotan is to feel the sting of his own wrong, and Brunhilde, his favorite child, shall become an unwilling but no less certain instrument to glut Fricka's hate. Standing for a while mute, hesitant,

THE VALKYRIE.

contemplating the fearful deed which she is bidden to perform, Brunhilde at length painfully gathers up her spear and shield and woefully utters

> "How heavy feels my weapons to raise them for a wrong.
> Though light they seem when for good cause I wield them.
> Abandon hope, then I may no longer succor
> Thy defender once; I must perforce forsake thee."

Thus speaking she turns away, but perceiving Siegmund and Sieglinda approaching she watches them a while, then proceeds to the cave where her horse is stabled from view.

Scene III.—Siegmund and Sieglinda now appear, well spent with fatigue by their flight from Hunding, who is in hot pursuit. As they stop on the mountain side Sieglinda faints from exhaustion, the scene being one of great power, in which voice and instrumentation portray the alternations of love and despair. Siegmund makes no attempt to restore her to consciousness, considering that it were better she should not be witness of the combat which is near at hand.

As the sound of Hunding's horn is heard in the distance, Brunhilde, the Valkyrie, appears before Siegmund with deepest melancholy marked upon her face, for she is come to warn him of his defeat and death. He courageously tells her of his matchless sword that shall win him the victory; but sorrowfully she answers that it shall not be so, for his sword will be shivered when most he needs it, but that consolation may be found, for though to death he is doomed, to Walhalla she will lead him, there to meet his father and participate forevermore in the joys of the gods. With passionate eagerness he inquires if he shall embrace Sieglinda in the halls of Walhalla, to which Brunhilde replies that it is decreed Sieglinda may not enter the abodes reserved for heroes; that he shall see her no more. Calmed by his great grief, Siegmund bends above the still unconscious form of his mistress sister, and planting a fervid kiss upon her brow, with marked tranquillity he turns to Brunhilde, saying:

> "Whether in bliss or shame Sieglinda bides,
> Siegmund will count it joy to share her fate."

Rousing again to face his foes, he asks by whom is it decreed that he shall fall, and when told that Hunding's sword will slay him, he valiantly pleads the power of his own good weapon and welcomes the fight. Thereupon Brunhilde, with emphasis, tells him of Wotan's order, that the charm shall be withdrawn which made his sword mighty in combats, and that it can avail him naught henceforth. At this revelation Siegmund, bending low above Sieglinda, in an outburst of agony pours out his complaint against a father who would bestow a sword of shifting shield, and declares that if he perish it will not be to pass to Walhalla, to be waited upon by the mist maidens of paradise, for to him companionship of gods were no requirement for the loss of Sieglinda. Better were it that Hella should hold him as her prey, than that Walhalla be gained with loss of one most dear. Brunhilde would shame him for rejecting celestial splendors for a faint and feeble woman, at which, with bitterness writ upon his countenance, he charges her with heartless contempt for his love, and bids her, if she cannot pity his despair, to freely feast upon his woe, but vaunt not to him of Walhalla's paltry virtues.

Brunhilde is moved to great compassion by Siegmund's distress, and beseeches that he give into her keeping the one he so devotedly loves, promising to shield her with all her power; but Siegmund will allow no one to afford protection, for such is his jealous devotion that rather than suffer Sieglinda to become the ward of another he threatens

THE VALKYRIE.

to slay her with his own hands, and bids his sword to execute his terrible purpose. Brunhilde interposes to prevent so dreadful an act, and in gust of sympathy she implores him to forbear, and listen to her voice. She now tells him that Sieglinda shall live, and he shall not leave her side; that in defiance of Wotan's command she will protect him. The horn of Hunding sounds in the distance again, at which, assuring him of her aid in the combat, Brunhilde disappears, with her horse, in the ravine, as the storm clouds gather and darkness descends upon the mountains.

Scene V.—When the light breaks, Siegmund is seen bending over Sieglinda in deepest anxiety, singing:

"The mask of death appears upon her face.
But living her heaving breast doth prove ;
So sleep in peace till the battle be won
And fate shall expose whom the victor has spoiled."

Then laying her gently upon a rocky shelf he kisses her a sad farewell as Hunding's horn sounds again, which challenge he hastens to meet by hurrying up the mountain steep, where he is soon hidden by inky clouds that are frequently riven by lightning flashes.

As Siegmund disappears Sieglinda is heard uttering, in her dreams, cries of fear, at visions of threatening strangers, of turbid vapors, and fiery tongues, rehearsing the scenes that attended the murder of her mother, the burning of her home, and her own captivity, by the cruel Hunding; and shrieking she calls, "Oh, help me, brother! Siegmund! Siegmund!" So terrifying has been her dream, so loud the thunder echoes, so violent the lightning's flash, that Sieglinda is awakened, to find herself alone, and her fright is increased by hearing a blast from Hunding's horn sounded near by, followed by his voice from a mountain peak shouting defiance, to which a bold challenge is flung back by Siegmund. The two have sought each other in the darkness, where by answering threat and war-cry they approach, and as the jagged rocks are lighted by dazzling flashes, Siegmund and Hunding are seen engaged in mortal combat. Sieglinda screams her beseechments to the men to stay their hands, begging that she may be murdered first, and makes an effort to reach the combatants, but a blinding flash of lightning sends her reeling, by the glare of which Brunhilde is discovered hovering over Siegmund, encouraging him to be firm of hand and fell of purpose. Thus the battle rages furiously with the wage favoring Siegmund, until a ruddy glow issues from the boiling storm-clouds, that reveals Wotan standing over Hunding warding the blows of Siegmund, and there is heard his ominous voice

"Recoil from my spear! Be splintered the sword!" As these dreadful words are spoken, Brunhilde flies in terror from her father down the rocks, and as Siegmund's sword is broken, Hunding plunges his spear into the breast of the now weaponless man.

Sieglinda has seen with horror the fatal thrust of Hunding, and falls fainting, but she is ministered to by Brunhilde, who tenderly conveys her away on her horse, at which moment the dark clouds divide and Hunding is revealed drawing his spear from Siegmund's breast.

Wotan has wrought this evil to his son by Fricka's jealous command, and now gazing painfully, remorsefully upon the stricken body he utters:

"Get hence (to Walhalla), knave, kneel before Fricka,
Tell her how Wotan's spear avenged his spouse's slight."

Hunding's victory over Siegmund is dearly purchased, for the sorrowful Wotan revenges the deed which his own hand, by compulsion, has accomplished. With a look of divine accusation he strikes the victor dead at his feet, but having thus wrought his vengeance upon Hunding, he turns his wrath upon Brunhilde for having violated the command he gave her, and with a threat to follow her for punishment, Wotan disappears, amid thunder and lightning, as the curtain falls.

ACT III, Scene I.—The next and concluding act of the opera opens with a scene of remarkable effectiveness, the influence of which is felt long after the music has departed from our memories. As the curtain rises there is discovered a plateau on a mountain peak, in the land of the gods, to which spot, called "Valkurfels," the Valkyries bear on winged steeds the bodies of the heroic slain for entrance to Walhalla. One by one the eight Valkyries come into view shouting their weird cries, and each with the corpse of a warrior, whose name they triumphantly announce. Last of all appears Brunhilde, carrying Sieglinda on her fleet horse Grani, who appeals to her sisters for their assistance in protecting her charge from the wrath of Wotan. When the others ask for explanation of Brunhilde's fears, she tells them hurriedly of the events of the day, and of how she has sought to shelter Siegmund even against the decree of Wotan, who now pursues in wrathful vengeance to punish her treason. The storm increases, and the danger grows. Her sisters refuse Brunhilde's appeals for help, fearful of their father's anger, nor will lend a horse in aid the escape of Sieglinda. While the Valkyrie is thus beseeching Sieglinda recovers consciousness, whereupon, appreciating her miserable situation, she reproaches Brunhilde for separating her from peril, since she might have died by the self-same spear that slew Siegmund, but since so dear a death cannot now be hers, she implores:

"A last prayer for your pity! Canst thou refuse?
With thy sword strike my heart, that my grief may be healed!"

Brunhilde is all compassion for Sieglinda's grief, but bids her be more courageous for another's sake.

"Desire not death, but keep life for that other
A pledge which thy husband sacredly gave
The babe which thou bearest, a Wolsung is he!"

Thus reminded of her unborn child, the mother instinct stifles despair, and she thus supplicates with voice of moving entreaty, mindful not of self but of that one which is to be

"Brave one, to my rescue!
Shield thou my babe
Maiden of war, grant me protection
A mother's heart appeals for your aid"

Brunhilde is unable to resist such prayerful pleadings, and raising Sieglinda up she bids her hasten her escape while she remains to hinder Wotan and receive his wrath. "Whence may I safely wander," eagerly Sieglinda inquires, to which Siegruna, one of the Valkyries, advises that she seek the tangled forest where the Nibelung's hoard Fafner has secreted,—Fafner the giant who has been changed to a dread dragon, and in a hole harbors with Alberich's ring. Here Wotan will not pursue, lest he fall under the curse of the mystic gold, and so Brunhilde urges Sieglinda to fly to these dread haunts, nor count her sufferings as aught since she as wife will gave birth to the greatest hero the world has known. Hastily she produces pieces of Siegmund's sword from under her breastplate, and giving these to Sieglinda admonishes her to keep them sacredly, for:

"This sword, reforged, he shall hereafter wield,
And know his name is—Siegfried, son of victry!"

Giving her blessings to the maiden divine, and confessing the comfort she has received, Sieglinda hurries away. The rocky peak now becomes enveloped in thunder clouds, the tempest roars, but above the stormy tumult the voice of Wotan is heard calling Brunhilde, who petitions her sister Valkyries for help. This they reluctantly grant by concealing her in their midst, but Wotan quickly detects her presence and rebuking the sisters for sheltering a culprit, he bids her forth for sentence. Brunhilde tremblingly obeys, and answers: "Here stand I, father, to suffer thy decree." With solemn speech the angered god recounts the acts of her disobedience; how she has faltered in her duties as wish-maid, shield-maid, and lot-chooser, for which offences she is banished from Walhalla; from her high estate as a Valkyrie to the slavish conditions and fretful limitations of a mortal: that she shall espouse a man born to an earth estate, and in becoming wife she shall endure the sorrows, disappointments, and all the painful experiences that fall to womankind.

THE VALKYRIE

So great a penalty no god before has pronounced, nor has mercy been so strained to punish disobedience of a command that outrages holy sentiment, yet while wounding himself, Wotan declares:

> "She must a consort receive like maid of the world.
> His commands to obey with good will.
> No more think of home among the gods of Valhall
> But as housewife her duties fulfil."

This dreadful sentence of disinheritance, which is banishment from bliss, and degradation, causes the goddess to sink upon her knees in despair as the Valkyries utter, "Horror! Woe! Sister! Oh, sister!" These beseech their father to mitigate his curse, reminding him that as sisters they must share her shame. But Wotan is inexorable, and lest they be tempted to succor her, he threatens them with direful punishment if they remain near her, or attempt to furnish help. The Valkyries now rush away, uttering cries of woe and sympathy for their condemned sister, whose compassionate deed has incurred their father's curse. The storm subsides, and as the clouds disperse, evening twilight falls.

Scene III.—The succeeding scene shows Brunhilde prostrate at the feet of Wotan. After a painful silence she slowly rises to a kneeling position and passionately pleads:

> "Was it so base a crime I did commit
> That I deserve a punishment so dire?
> I beseech thee father, on bended knee behold
> Thy daughter, whom thou once loved, pleading for mercy.
> Wreak not shore ire, but make to me clear the mortal
> Guilt that with cruel firmness compels thee to
> Cast off thy favorite child."

The shadow of menace on Wotan's brows is not dispelled by Brunhilde's agony, and gloomily he repels her beseechments by asking her to consider her deed, which must show the guilt that deserves his reprobation. She will not be thus cast off without excusing her offending, and failing to arouse his compassion, Brunhilde reminds her father that she has executed his decree in protecting Siegmund, which though revoked, it was through influence of Fricka's hatred of his son, which made him false to himself; wherefore she had held his true wish in shielding Siegmund. To this moving argument she adds how sight of Siegmund, and his devotion to Sieglinda, had excited her pity, a feeling which she has inherited, and therefore she was most faithful to her father when thwarting his cruel command, for her heart has taught her "to love all that thou didst love."

Wotan manifests contrition, and feels a woe for that which Fricka has compelled him to do, but his decrees are binding, unless absolved by one of equal power, and so he may not revoke the sentence which he has uttered, even though against his child. Brunhilde, thereupon bowing her resignation, conjures her father that since she is to be consigned to the earth, to the life of a mortal, to bear all the pains and disappointments which belong to woman, she may not become wife of a worthless churl, but of one who by courage and worth may win her love, for:

> Once thou mad'st thou a glorious breed
> No mean one shall ever debase it!
> One valiant over all I vouch it.
> Shall spring from Wolsung's line."

Wotan is impatient at such allusion to the Wolsung line, which is harrowing to his remembrance, for by the death of Siegmund accomplished in his wrath, all hope of an heir to bear the Wolsung name is forever destroyed. Brunhilde cautions that it may not be so, since Sieglinda, sister, yet wife, to Siegmund, has been preserved, and she guardeth the sword that was shaped for victory. Wotan, in boastful speech, reminds her that on the mountain peak, when Hunding's spear opposed the sword of Siegmund, the magic weapon was broken, and scornfully asks, "Who may now

THE VALKYRIE.

restore and wield it?" The exultant tones in which her father recites the triumph of his will, the consummated crime that jealous Fricka has inspired, cause her to realize the futility of her persuasion, the hopelessness of her opposition to the divine decree, wherefore yielding her allegiance, and accepting the fate that Wotan would impose, Brunhilde falls on her knees and prayerfully entreats:

> "Must I be bound by gyves of wakeless sleep
> Till roused to be a prey to some wanton churl?
> If thou wilt helpless make me, one 'quest I pray:
> My form, I beg, be hedged about with hind'ring dread,
> Until waked I may be by a fearless man,
> Who would dangers dare to win a faithful heart.
> By thy command may flames of quenchless fire
> Wall me within 'gainst cowardly intruders.
> To destroy with fiercest tongue, and rend with hate
> Whoso unworthy would seize me for a prize!'"

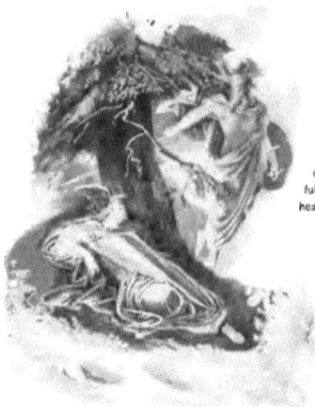

Touched by her petition, and sorrowing for the deed that reft him of a son, Wotan promises to yield to her request, and he sings a mournful farewell which is one of the gems of the lyric drama. Clasping her head in both his hands his song concludes with the painful words:

> "With heart rent of grief thy father giveth his kiss,
> But though sorrowing, he taketh thy godhood away."

As Wotan presses a lingering kiss on Brunhilde's eyes, she sinks in his arms, her powers of godhood slowly departing. When she becomes unconscious he tenderly disposes her on a mossy mound, shaded by an overspreading fir-tree, carefully closes her helmet, and then covers her body with the gleaming shield of the Valkyrie. Having thus consigned the sleeper, Wotan moves slowly away, casting lingering looks behind, until reaching the centre of the stage he thrusts his spear into the earth beside a large rock, and thus exorcising the god of fire, he speaks:

> "Loki, hear! Listen and heed!
> When first I found thee thou wert but a glow,
> Upon which I breathed the breath of fire.
> When as a flame I seized and bound thee.
> To my service now! Spread thy mantle round
> And shield her with thy protecting arms;
> Loki! Loki! I command thee appear!"

As these words are spoken, a stream of fire issues from about the rock, which grows rapidly until, leaping high and spreading, the flames surround Wotan, who now directs that they encircle the precipice and be a permanent wall to protect Brunhilde until she be wakened by one who hath the courage of a god, and all the virtues of mortals. Then casting a last, lingering look at his brave and beautiful child, once the light and life of his heart, he disappears through the fire, and the curtain descends.

Siegfried

SIEGFRIED—"*Look out, growler, the booster comes!*
There lie, noisome rogue!
Needful sticks in your gizzard!"

ACT II.—SCENE VI.

SIEGFRIED.

UR appreciation of the melodic germ of the trilogy becomes accentuated by the second division of the great drama, for though there is evident intimation of the author-composer's purpose in the "Rhinegold" and "Valkyrie," the full idealization appears, and the allegory becomes clear in the story of "Siegfried." In the days of barbarism men were governed in nearly all their acts by superstitions, and these vain beliefs became living forces through the individual attributes—personification—which the infantile mind of early man attached to all natural impulses as well as to powers that reside within the elements. Good and evil were also represented as being in eternal conflict, as were the spirits of light and darkness, and of ignorance and intelligence. These contending powers are allegorically treated, the moral of which is gradually revealed by the progress of the story.

In the "Valkyrie" Wagner had to deal chiefly with the elemental forces, with the storm, combats, war-cries, and tumultuous passions, but in "Siegfried" there succeeds a grateful repose and serenity that befits the birth of love, and the stages that lead to beneficent attainments. These varying scenes, that blend the human with the divine, Wagner simulated by instrumentation, and interpreted by poetic description, little short of the marvelous, and the wonder grows rather than lessens with age, through the frequent but always feeble efforts of imitators.

The opening of the opera of "Siegfried" does not directly connect with the close of the "Valkyrie," an omission which it is necessary to supply by the following:

When Sieglinda, to escape the ire of Wotan, fled to the dense coverts, she wandered aimlessly about for a while until, fairly spent with hunger and fatigue, she came upon the cavern home of Mime, the dwarf brother of Alberich, who, taking pity upon her miserable condition, consented to receive her. Here she remained, in the dark recesses of Mime's cave, until her appointed time arrived, when she gave birth to a son, whom she named Siegfried, as Brunhilde had foretold. So great had been her sorrows and exposures, added to the pains of parturition, that she was unable to survive her afflictions, and feeling that death was approaching, in her last moments she consigns the care of her babe to the dwarf, which responsibility he assumes with satisfaction, foreknowing the abilities which the child will develop, which he hopes to employ to recover the magical ring wrested from him through the cunning of Loki and Wotan.

Siegfried grows to lusty manhood, strong, sinewy, and fearless; a bold woodsman, indefatigable in the chase, and as a hunter he ranges the forests, holding the fiercest animals at his will, and is able to imitate the cries of all birds and beasts of the woods. His free life and conquests over nature inspire him to loftier deeds, to heroic acts, and he conceives a higher passion which, though indistinct, and to his perceptions indefinable, is still directive, filling his mind with visions, and he longs to learn of the world that lies beyond the horizon of his small experience. Moved by this shapeless ambition, Siegfried questions Mime of the peoples and powers of the earth, and would learn something respecting his birth and heritage. To these inquiries the dwarf answers him by relating how his mother died, committing him to his care, but leaving no other legacy than the fragments of his father's sword that had been shivered by Wotan's spear. These, however, are the broken bits of a marvelous weapon, and that if any one succeeds in forging therefrom a new sword, by its aid the power will be given to conquer every opposing thing or obstacle. Mime is a blacksmith, whose cunning skill made the magic cap and the mystic ring, so Siegfried sets him to the task of recasting and forging a perfect sword from the pieces, though it has been told this can be accomplished by no other than he who is a hero destitute of fear.

Act I, Scene I.—The first scene of the opera represents the workshop of Mime, a dark cave with an opening towards the wood. Against the wall is a forge formed of stones, from which rises a rough chimney, and in front is a large anvil with smithy tools scattered about. When the curtain is lifted, after a short orchestral prelude, Mime is seen hammering a sword on the anvil; but after delivering a few blows he sings his discouragement at shaping a sword so often which the young stripling (Siegfried) always twists in two as 'twere a straw. After cogitating for a while, the dwarf recites to himself, that there is a blade which if made from the fragments of Nothung (signifying "needful"), the sword that Siegmund wore, no one may break it, and such a weapon, if he but had the skill to weld it, would pay him well for his pains. At thought of what may be gained thereby Mime is encouraged to resume his work, for it is by such a sword Fafner, the dragon, who guards the Nibelung's gold, may be destroyed and the treasure recovered. His prescience enables him to know that Siegfried will win this victory, and he counts on becoming master of the mystic hoard when the fearsome guardian is slain. Resolutely he hammers and files the broken sword, encouraging himself with expectations of his great reward, an attainment of his ambition for wealth and power, but the steel is refractory and yields nothing to his efforts, until, spent with labor, he grows hopeless of the task and despondently utters

"Take him away." Say piteously sport

— I knock and I hammer.
But at the boy's behest,
He'll bend and snap it in two,
Yet scolds if I cease to forge."

At this juncture Siegfried enters the cave, clothed with animal skins and wearing a silver horn slung by a chain at his side. Following him is a bear, which he has caught and bridled, and leading the beast into the dwarf's presence he roughly urges it to attack him. Mime trembles with terror, and seeks escape by crouching behind his anvil, when, with shouts of laughter, Siegfried bids the bear ask for the sword, at which the dwarf piteously declares he has cast the weapon fit and fairly this day. Being told that the sword is fashioned, Siegfried abates his assumed anger and loosing the bear drives it into the wood, then sits down to recover from his laughter. Suddenly he jumps up again and receives the sword from Mime's trembling hand, which he shivers by a stroke on the anvil, and follows the act with bitter revilings of the dwarf, whose work is always disappointing.

Mime, plucking up courage under Siegfried's berating, charges him with ingratitude, in being mindless of the loving care he has given since motherless he was committed to his keep. Siegfried turns away sulkily, impatient of such reminder, whereupon to regain his favor Mime brings soup and meat which he condescendingly offers, but Siegfried impetuously strikes the food from his hand saying, "Meals I make for myself; you can swill your slop alone."

Mime is much hurt by Siegfried's insult, and upbraids him roundly for his ill requital of the devotion lavished upon him, and so speaking falls to sobbing. Siegfried feels no compunction under the dwarf's just accusing, but his irritation rather increases, and gazing steadily in Mime's face he expresses the passions that ebb and flow tumultuously in his bosom, prompting ever to a desire which he cannot define, and thus he unbosoms himself of his longings

> "If you have wisdom
> Then read me wisely
> A thing I have pored upon.
> When I seek the forest to escape you,
> What motive makes me return?
> Not a beast but I love better than you;
> If you've a mind, then tell me why I return?"

Affectionately, Mime assures Siegfried that these are but the natural longings of youth, the proofs that young ones need always the parents' nest. What the father is to the fledgling, such Mime declares is his own faithful cherishing of his foster son. This speech begets Siegfried's curiosity, which he betrays by asking the motive of love-life; why the birds mate and joy in their brood; the animals of the forest consort and live in mutual love with their offspring, and yet he hath not had that which child may cherish:

> "A querulous brat kindly you learnt,
> Wrapped in warm linen the little wretch;
> How came you then to possess me?
> Was I without mother made?"

Mime tries to console Siegfried by asserting that he is both mother and father in one, but the young hero resents such claim, calling Mime perfidious fool to tell him a lying thing, for 'twere as true to compare a toad with a fish, and a toad ne'er had fish for father. With show of great vexation, Siegfried declares that now he has discovered what power it is that brings him home; what prompting it is that draws him to a cave where love hath no abiding:

> "It is to make you tell me.
> What father and mother are mine!"

When Mime shrinks with appearance of amazement at such question, Siegfried seizes him by the throat and refuses to release his crushing grasp until the hideous dwarf signifies his consent to tell the hero's parentage. Thereupon Mime admits that he is no father, and repeats the story of how he found Sieglinda in the wood and helped her to his cave, where soon she bore a babe, and dying gave the child to him for rearing. Urged to speak further, the dwarf tells the name of mother and babe: Sieglinda the parent, Siegfried the offspring; since which time he has been mother and father in one to the child now reared to lusty manhood.

Siegfried, eager to hear more, but ever doubting, demands to know what name his father bore, at which Mime vows that he has heard no other word than that some one slew him, for so the mother with dying breath had told that her child was fatherless. Siegfried is so dissatisfied with the dwarf's reply that he demands presentment of some evidence of what is declared, whereat Mime, with show of hesitation, produces two pieces of a sword, saying:

> "This had I of thy mother.
> For message tell and trouble.
> Was it my scant reward.
> See here but a broken sword!
> She said thy father had swung it
> At the fight in which he was killed."

It is the relics of the good sword Needful, which with new forging may conquer all adversaries, and in exultation Siegfried commands the dwarf to make a new weapon of the pieces, threatening punishment if he fails. Much frightened by the hero's manner, Mime asks what he has a mind to do, to which Siegfried replies that his purpose is to wander far and return no more; since father and mother he has none, he will seek another home than that which has known his youth; and without further

"Oho! Oho! Oho!
Sharp are the thy hammer, a hardy fellow."

speech he hastens away into the wood, leaving the dwarf a prey to astonishment. In profoundest meditation Mime considers what he may do to assist Siegfried to engage the dragon Fafner; how first to forge the stubborn steel of Needful, which resists the fiercest furnace heat and defies his cunning to weld its broken parts. Confessing his hopelessness of accomplishing the task which Siegfried has appointed, Mime crouches down despairingly behind his anvil, but is quickly aroused by the entrance of Wotan, who, with spear in hand, and slouch hat drawn low to hide his missing eye, hails the dwarf as wisest of smiths and craves his hospitality. Mime is much startled by the manner of this strange self-invited guest, and asks his name and intent, at which Wotan calls himself "Wanderer," because he has roamed the wide-world over, doing such deeds as made men wonder, gathering treasure, and giving wisdom to the witless. Mime has no mind to entertain so strange a person, but Wotan, marking the dwarf's fright and perplexity, makes bold to seat himself at the hearth, and with some bravado challenges Mime to a struggle of wits in which heads shall be the stakes, promising to sacrifice his own if a question be asked which he is unable to answer. Hoping to entrap Wotan,—confiding in his artfulness, even though it served him fruitlessly when matched with

that of Alberich,—Mime accepts the gage, upon condition that his visitor shall first give true replies to these three inquiries:
"Now, read me aright. What race is born in the earth's deep bowels?"
"What race is it, I pray you tell me, that liveth upon the surface of the world?"
"Lastly; who is it that wards the heavens above?"
To these the cunning god, Wotan, now the Wanderer, makes his truthful answers:
"In the earth there burrow the Nibelungs, black gnomes by Alberich once governed, who by the spell of a magic ring did move the dwarfs to industry in heaping up endless hoards of riches wherewith to win the world.
"Upon the world's great back there lived the fearsome giants, Fasolt and Fafner, who so envied Alberich his wealth that they ravished first his magic ring, then fell to quarreling over the hoard they gained, till Fafner slew his brother, and now, changed to dragon, doth guard the golden treasure."

To the third he thus makes answer: "The welkin above is Walhalla, where Wotan ruleth. Once from the world's ash tree he fashioned a mighty spear, around the shaft of which he graved magic runes, and to its power both Nibelungs and giants bow, for to such spear they allegiance must confess."

As if by accident, Wotan sets his spear upon the ground, when forthwith a peal of thunder follows, at which Mime manifests much terror. Wotan has answered the three questions truly and saved his forfeit, and now he demands his right to similarly propound as many riddles. The dwarf is in panic at the evil prospect of his failure to answer well, but he may not shrink now from fulfilling the conditions which he himself named, and so tremblingly he promises to reply.

"Now, amiable dwarf, what noble race is it that Wotan harshly dealt with, and yet deemeth

most dear, they who have felt the weight of his anger, but who receiveth the love of a parent pitying his corrected child?"

"It was the Wolsungs," answers the dwarf, "a valued race indeed, which Wotan fathered, but from whom his favor did withdraw. Siegmund and Sieglinda sprang from these, a turbulent pair, but they were father and mother of Siegfried, the bravest of the Wolsung breed.

"Thou answereth truly the primal riddle; a wily Nibelung wardeth Siegfried, fated slayer of Fafner, but it is that he may himself possess the magic ring and all the treasure. But what sword must Siegfried wield to slay this giant dragon?"

Mime is all eagerness to give his reply, so easy is the riddle of solution, and so he promptly answers "Needful is the sword which Wotan struck into an ash tree and gave to him who might draw it forth. Full many strove, but only Siegmund, the warlike, won the prize and wore it well in strife till by Wotan's spear 'twas shivered. Now a subtle smith doth preserve the parts, which, firmly forged anew, may destroy the dragon who guards the magic treasure."

"So well dost thou unravel my questions that wisdom such as thine may rarely be found," encourages Wotan, "but one other yet remains, and if thou shalt answer this as wittily I will acquit thee and save thy head. Say, then, thou wise smith, who is it that from the pieces will forge anew the good sword Needful?"

At this question Mime starts in greatest terror, for he has exhausted his skill in vain efforts to weld the broken blade, as flux and solder fail to melt the steel, and hammer and anvil, under stoutest arms, make no impression upon the obstinate pieces. Frankly, at last, Mime confesses he cannot shape the sword, and piteously asks how this secret may be discovered. Wotan, as Wanderer, rises from the hearth with show of anger, and reminds the dwarf how his failure to resolve the question has lost him his head, but satisfied to see the dwarf cringing with terror, Wotan disdains to exact the forfeit, and tells him that none who hath ever been moved by fear may restore the sword Needful, and laughing at Mime's fright, he retires into the forest.

For a while after Wotan's departure, the dwarf gazes fixedly from behind his anvil towards the woods, where beholding a dreadful vision of Fafner, the dragon, which he believes is about to devour him, he shrieks with fright and cowers out of sight, as Siegfried calls from without. "Ho! lazy fellow, have you finished the sword?" Siegfried now enters the cave, and hunts the dwarf from his hiding place, demanding again if he has forged the blade! Mime begs for mercy, excusing his poor cunning which cannot mend the sword, that for wit to know his head has been forfeit to him who has not learned to fear. Siegfried seizes Mime violently and bids him tell what thing it was that made him crouch with fright, at which the dwarf declares it is the dread that he would teach, since the firmest sword is potent only in the hands of him who knows not fear. "If it is an art," impatiently inquires Siegfried, "why am I untaught; why have you not instructed me that I may fear?" With great animation the dwarf asks Siegfried if in the forest dark, at gloaming hour, when with rush and roar fearful hurtlings swell and surge, to dazzle, flicker and swoop, no grisly gruesomeness has filled his fancy? Siegfried answers that he has never listened to such sounds, nor felt a quaking, and seeks to experience a feeling that will make his heart beat with alarm.

"If you would know the pangs of fear," the dwarf addresses, "follow me well to Hate-cavern, which lieth close at hand, wherein reposes a monstrous dragon that hath devoured many folk; fear thou'lt learn from Fafner, if thou wilt approach his hole." Siegfried rejoices at this chance of schooling, which leads towards the outer world much longed for, and hastily he bids the dwarf shape the sword, that he may go forth to test its steel upon the dragon. With whimpering words Mime tells again his inability to weld the obstinate pieces, which none may do save he who hath never felt the sensation of fear.

Siegfried rails at the dwarf as bungler and deceiver, and ends his tirade by commanding that the bits of blade be brought, that he himself will essay to shape the sword. The furnace thereupon is fed with coal, the bellows worked till the fire is fierce, and when the heat is greatest Siegfried adjusts the pieces of blade in a vise and files them to a dust which he places in a crucible on the forge and by briskly working the bellows reduces it to molten metal. Carefully then he casts the weapon, after which he hammers the blade into perfect shape, meanwhile lustily singing the sword song, "Needful, Needful, notable sword," the motive of which is supplied in "The Rhinegold," and which is one of the favorite numbers of the "Trilogy."

While Siegfried is singing at his work, Mime is engaged contriving means by which he may gain possession of the all-conquering sword; and gaily he sings a disclosure of his purpose to mix a poison portion that he may induce Siegfried to drink, whereby a triumph to achieve. In rapture, as his plans mature, the dwarf tells how he will secure the magic ring, when Fafner falls by Siegfried's stroke, with which possessed he will become lord of the Nibelungs, and with riches in full store both men and gods will do his bidding, and he will be acknowledged the mighty monarch, prince of earth-gnomes, ruler of all!

As Mime concludes his song, Siegfried finishes the sword and fixes the blade in its handle, whereupon he pours out his voice in triumphant melody and praise of the weapon, and as he ends he tests the steel by striking it with great violence upon the anvil, which is split in twain, and the parts fall with a great noise. Mime is terrified by this marvelous display of force, and throws himself prostrate upon the ground, while Siegfried brandishes his irresistible blade aloft and shouts with glee, as the curtain descends upon the first act.

The scenes attending the forging of the sword are almost incomparably grand, but equally effective is the instrumentation, that with wonderful realism imitates the roar of the forge, the snapping of flames, the sharp grating sound of filing steel, the hissing of water as the glowing blade is cooled, and the ringing blows upon the anvil.

Act II.—When the curtain rises again, a deep forest is shown, in the midst of which is the mouth of a vast cavern, while at one side is a fissured rocky cliff, against which Alberich is seen leaning in gloomy meditation. Alberich, brother of Mime, and former master, stands guard night and day before the cave where Fafner, the dragon, holds the treasure—the magic ring, the helmet of invisibility, and the vast store of gold. As Alberich sings of his duties, and anticipates the death of Fafner, Wotan appears, upon whose figure a burst of moonlight falls, which thus revealing him the dwarf breaks into imprecations, and pronouncing him villain, orders Wotan to quickly depart. When Wotan courageously asks who will bar his way, Alberich laughs spitefully and admonishes him to beware, for though his cunning once availed to wrest the ring, and his spear is writ with mystic runes, he dares not juggle with the giant, before whose power his spear will split like straw, like a javelin of glass struck upon a shield of steel, breaking to the touch; that Fafner, at once giant and dragon, mighty of strength, puissant with deadly breath and claw, now guards the store, through whom it will descend again to a Nibelung, whose stratagems will trick even monster and man. Thus boasting his artful wiles, the dwarf vaunts his purpose when the ring shall be his:

"I'll use the jewel's power,
Then tremble, thou high
Protector of heroes,
For Walhalla
I'll seize on with Hella's host,
And the world will then be mine."

Wotan charges Alberich to hold his wrath against him, as he will have cause to wrangle with Mime, who will soon bring a foe, even a boy, who without help from him will destroy the dragon, who it were best should be apprised of the strife that must now quickly follow, and luck be with the winner. Thereupon Wotan wakes the dragon, who growling cries, "Who stirs me from sleep?" Wotan answers, "It is a friend, come to warn thee of danger, but life I will allow thee for the treasure that thou holdeth." Alberich adds his warning too of a stalwart hero who approaches, and begs possession of the ring to keep until the strife be ended. Fafner, the dragon, replies that his maw yawns for a hero, and in fancied security he falls asleep.

Wotan laughs loudly, and counsels Alberich to guard well, "for what further befalls thou shalt quickly find." So saying, Wotan retires to the wood, and Alberich renews his watch, and his hopes as well to regain the ring. Morning dawns, and the entering beams of day light up the rocks, in a cleft of which Alberich hides as Mime and Siegfried cautiously approach.

Siegfried takes his station under a great lime tree, and Mime seats himself opposite, to watch the cave in which, he cautions Siegfried, lives the gruesome dragon, savage and monstrous, who has devoured many and has ever growing appetite for more; whose breath is poison, shriveling body and bones; whose twisting tail hath a grip to grind; whose body is cuirassed like a knight, and whose claws are stronger than daggers of steel. Siegfried is so little alarmed by these grisly descriptions that, indifferent to its power to harm, he asks, "Hath this dragon a heart, and doth a beat in place where lieth heart of other beasts?"

Mime answers, "Aye, a cruel and hardened heart; but hast thou not yet learned to fear?"

But heeding not the dwarf's alarms Siegfried promises that Needful shall find the dragon's heart, if heart he hath, and hew its way to victory, in which fight he needs no help and bids the dwarf to go hence, and leave him to battle alone. But Mime hesitates to leave, hoping still to inspire the hero with fear, and dwells upon the dragon's fearsome aspect, until, his patience gone, Siegfried fiercely repels the importunate and pestering dwarf:

"Forth from the sight of me begone,
This nuisance I'll no longer endure!"

Mime consents to take his leave, but with assumed solicitude he cautions Siegfried to be wary of the dragon, admonishing again that the worm is not easy to be vanquished, by knight however valiant; though if he be resolved to fight so fearsome a foe Mime warns that the dragon will leave his lair at noon-time and pass this way seeking the fountain for drink. As he hobbles off, in an aside he mutters, "Fafner and Siegfried—Siegfried and Fafner—would each the other might kill!" When Mime disappears, Siegfried seats himself again under the lime tree, and in thoughtful

silence muses upon his birth, striving to imagine the appearance of his father and mother, and expressing thanks that he is not son of one so hideous as Mime. While thus engaged with his thoughts, an increased rustling of the trees directs his attention to the branches and to the songs of birds, whose notes are surprisingly imitated by the orchestra. He recalls a prophecy one day made him by the dwarf, that he who attains the language of birds, interpreting their voices, may gain victories beyond the dreams of men. Forthwith he conceives the purpose of striving to discover the significance of their notes by imitating their music on a reed, which he fashions into a pipe, but repeated effort ends in failure, and throwing away the reed he blows a shrill call on his silver horn.

At the sound of Siegfried's horn Fafner emerges from his lair, and crawls upon a knoll, where he utters a savage growl. Siegfried laughs at the beast's monstrous length and horrible aspect, and humorously exclaims: "At last my notes have waked a fair-favored friend!" The dragon, which has the power of speech, languidly inquires, "What is that?" whereat Siegfried tells him that a beast with tongue of man may surely teach him something, and defiantly asks, "Mayhap I'll learn from thee what it is to fear?"

Fafner laughs, and showing his teeth and cavernous maw, remarks that, seeking water, good food he has found! and lashing his tail menacingly advances for the feast, but valiantly Siegfried draws his sword and confronts the monster. Fafner shoots a stream of poisonous flames at his adversary, which Siegfried avoids by springing aside, and as the dragon strikes with his tail Siegfried leaps over his back and wounds it with his sword. Doubly enraged by his hurt Fafner raises his body to deliver a crushing blow with his mighty, dagger-armed claws, thus exposing his breast, whereat with agile movement and dexterous thrust Siegfried plunges his sword to the very hilt into the heart of the beast, and leaving his weapon in the wound springs aside as the dragon with mighty roar falls in mortal throes.

With weakened voice, the dying monster summons strength to tell the story of how by slaying Fasolt he obtained the magic ring, thus triumphing o'er all the gods to gain a treasure, which to him who doth possess it brings naught but fatal ills. In admiration of the courage of a juvenile hero. Fafner is so magnanimous in the hour of his defeat as to warn Siegfried against the treason schemes of Mime and of Alberich, who have plotted his death that thereby they may acquire the treasure which though giving power hath wrought great woe.

Siegfried, believing that the dragon must have a knowledge of all things, tries to learn something of his parentage, but the request is made too late, for as the monster utters the word "Siegfried," he expires, rolling over on his side. Siegfried now draws his sword from the wound, and from the wound a flow of blood follows, some of which falls on the hero's hand, burning like fire. Instinctively, Siegfried lifts his hand to his mouth to suck the smarting blood. A moment later, to his amazement, he is enabled to interpret the language of birds, whose songs become as intelligible to him as the voice of human, and listening intently he hears a wood pecker singing in the lime tree:

"Hey! Siegfried shall now possess the Nibelung's hoard. If he gain the tarnhelm (magic helmet), wonderful things he shall achieve; but if the magic ring he ravishes, 'twill give him the ward of the world." Thankful for the bird's advice, he proceeds immediately to follow it by descending into the cavern in quest of the treasure.

As Siegfried disappears Mime sinks out of his place of hiding to assure himself of Fafner's death. At the same moment Alberich comes out of a cleft on the opposite side and watches Mime intently, until seeing he is about to enter the cave, he rushes in front and bars his way. The two now engage in a violent dispute over possession of the treasure, each claiming it by right, until Siegfried reappears bearing the magic gold, at which the dwarfs in fear hide themselves quickly. Fancying himself alone, Siegfried looks reflectively upon the tarnhelm and ring, wondering how he may best use them, when the bird-voice from the lime tree again admonishes: "Siegfried doth hold the helm and ring, but he may not trust Mime, the treacherous e'f." At the same moment Mime slowly approaches, speaking to himself of the wiles he has devised whereby to trap the truculent boy, and by his death gain all the treasure. Advancing nearer he asks Siegfried if the dragon he has really slain and learned what fear is? To this the hero makes answer that the monster was a foul-sort of fiend easily vanquished, for whom now he has a pity, since greater scoundrels, who directed his steps to the cave, are still living. Mime beastfully remarks that the conqueror of Fafner shall soon have his eyes closed in endless sleep, for all has been accomplished that he had sought, and the easy fool shall now surrender the treasure. "You are seeking to work my death, then," remarks Siegfried. "Thou shalt die, Siegfried, my son, if thou wilt not peacefully relinquish to me the golden hoard; for I have ever hated thy kind and fostered thee only that by thy service I might win the gold," replies the malignant and covetous dwarf.

"That you should hate me, gives me no disquiet, but must my life to you be delivered?" is Siegfried's answer; at which Mime perceives he has spoken too boldly, and by servile speech, and simulation of unctuous generosity, he disclaims such evil intent, declaring that it is not his life he seeks, but desire to warn him against a woeful fate that prompts his austere words. Then, soothingly, and sympathetically, the dwarf continues:

> "See, thou art tired with mighty toil,
> And burneth thy body with heat;
> So, to restore thee with stirring drink,
> Swiftly I have come to thee.
> While thy sword thou didst beat out
> I brewed this excellent stuff.
>
> (*To himself*) Take but a sip, I win thy trusty sword
> And with it the golden hoard and helm."

Mime draws near to Siegfried, and presses upon him a drinking horn, into which he has poured a poison draught, but his purpose being understood, through the warnings of the wood-pecker, Siegfried quickly draws his sword, and with one stroke lays the treacherous dwarf dead, then throws the body into the cave and stops the opening with the dragon's carcass. Returning again to the lime-tree he casts himself beneath its shade and resumes his musings, grieving that fortune has been so unkind as to leave him without mother, father, sister or brother, but committed him to the keep of a cankerous dwarf, who, foul of feature, has proved traitorous of soul; thereupon looking upward, he appeals to the bird to vouchsafe to him one gracious friend. The wood-pecker immediately replies:

> "Siegfried has slain the sinister dwarf!
> I wot for him now a glorious wife,
> In guarded fastness though she sleeps,
> Begirt about with fiercest flames.
> He who hath not fear and shall dare the blaze to pass
> To wake the sleeper there within
> Brunhilde for a bride shall win."

This song awakes in Siegfried the sentiment of love, which he has never felt before, and in exultation at the promise the bird to show him the path. As the bird flutters before, Siegfried hastens after, and as he disappears in the wood the second act concludes.

Act III.—When the curtain again rises, the audience beholds a wild region of gorge and mountain, wrapped in the shades of night, and rent by thunder and lightning. Before a cavernous hollow in the rocks Wotan, the Wanderer, is seen, conjuring Erda to appear. In response to the words of enchantment the gorge glows with light, and the goddess rises enveloped in an opalescent halo, and robed in gleaming garments that are covered with frost. Asking why she is summoned, Wotan invokes her prescient knowledge to foretell to him what the future holds, and how the prophesied downfall of the gods may be averted; to which she answers, by repeating how Brunhilde has been doomed to sleep in fire-surrounded bed, and warns that one who hath not felt the sense of fear, shall soon awaken and claim her for bride, but cannot tell him more. As Erda sinks into the earth the gorge grows dark again, but the storm subsides and a rising moon flooding the wood with light reveals the approach of Siegfried, who enters bewildered because the bird has disappeared, and he believes he must seek the sleeping Brunhilde without further aid. Wotan emerges from his retreat, sullen and impassioned, who perceiving Siegfried struggling in pensive mood, rudely accosts him with a challenge to know what motive brings him into this storm-riven wood. Siegfried, with heart set upon the enterprise that promises to gain

94   SIEGFRIED.

for him the hand and heart of one who will teach him the art of love and afford fulfillment of his ardent aspirations, speaks
to himself, "I hear a voice; will he tell me the way?" and then eagerly answers:

<blockquote>
"For a rock I am seeking,
Around which fire doth circle,
Where sleeps a woman I fain would wake!"
</blockquote>

A long dialogue ensues, in which Siegfried tells how he slew the monster Fafner, and
by taste of the dragon's blood has become gifted with a knowledge of bird language, through which
direction he has come to seek the fire-encircled woman who is to be his wife. Wotan bars his
progress, which so enrages Siegfried that, discovering his opponent has lost one eye, he threatens
to pruck out the other. This defiance arouses Wotan's wrath, who tells the impetuous youth
that the bird which he has followed has fled to save its life, and that the way which it
had pointed he shall not pass, for whoso wakes the maid and win her shall destroy forever
all power of the gods. He then points with spear towards the glowing vapors that rise about
Brunhilde, and warns Siegfried against attempting to pass the fiery barrier. This counsel
nerves Siegfried to quickly pursue his venture and he advances towards the furnace, whereupon
Wotan stretches out his spear and threatens that if fire doth not appall, his good weapon shall
not spare to punish his reckless purpose.

Siegfried draws his sword, and with ferocious blow shivers the spear, at which Wotan
recoils, confessing his defeat, saying, "Advance, I cannot prevent thee." The stage
suddenly becomes illuminated, as by a rolling sea of fire. Siegfried blows a blast upon
his horn, and then plunges into the flames, which so completely envelop him that his
form is hidden, but his course is indicated by the sounding of his horn, first near,
then further away, indicating his ascent of the mountain. Presently the glow subsides, and as the flame and vapor disappear, a clear blue sky is seen above a
lofty peak, as in the "Valkyrie." At the base of a wide-spreading fir-tree lies
Brunhilde, in a suit of plate armor, on her head a helmet, and over her body is spread
a long shield, and beyond, a little way, is her war horse, waiting in tranquil sleep. Siegfried
approaches, and discovering the sleeping woman, he advances quickly, lifts the shield, unfastens the helmet which has
concealed her features, and seeing her beauty thus revealed, he starts in rapture! With tender care he cuts the rings
of mail, and lifting the corselet and greaves, there lies before him the beautiful woman of his dreams. His heart which
has been a stranger to fear begins now to beat with wild tremulousness, a passion which, born of God, is developed by
the holy influence of sex affinity, and thus enthralled by its power, he sinks his head upon Brunhilde's bosom, crying

<blockquote>
"Mother, mother, how mighty thy son!
A woman folded in sleep
At last has enslaved him with fear."
</blockquote>

Breaking into song of delight, Siegfried imprints a kiss upon Brunhilde's lips, whose eyes open in astonishment.
She recognizes him as the lover she has awaited, and a long dialogue of exquisite song succeeds, in which Brunhilde
declares, that though she must lose her divine nature by loving and being loved of a mortal, she yields with joy, even at
the sacrifice of Walhalla, and annihilation of the gods, for the world were well lost for the kingdom of love which she has
won. Throwing herself into Siegfried's arms, they embrace each other passionately, and thus the act is ended.

Gotterdammerung

(AFTER THE ORIGINAL PAINTING BY FRED LEEKE)

GUTRUNE — *"Welcome, O guest,*
To Gibich's house!
From its daughter take thou the drink

ACT I.

DIE GOTTERDAMMERUNG
(DOWNFALL OF THE GODS.)

GRAND, aye, sublime as are the first three sections of Wagner's festival-acting drama, Buhnenfestspiel, as he was most pleased to call the tetralogy, that of the conclusion is transcendent, as it is most spectacular, composing a befitting climax to the fundamental themes embodied in the story.

Quite twenty-five years were required to adapt his artistic ideas to a perfect poetical-musical form, a period which though not wholly occupied by the actual labor of composition, yet represented the time it took to develop the conception into an instructive, allegoric, lyric drama, with all the accessories necessary to an effective rendition.

It is needful to appreciate that the trilogy, so far from being a mere play of the imagination, romantically and fantastically woven for theatrical exhibition, is in fact a personification of moral principles with which the human race, in its cultured divisions, is vitally concerned. The four dramas are inseparable, for they form a single great tragedy, which is intended to show how the destinies of gods and men are closely linked by common guilt and common expiation. Siegfried is identified with Baldur, the god of spring, and his death is a symbol of human fate, as well also the destruction of the race (myths) of the gods. Throughout the dramatic representation, we cannot fail to observe how ambition for power and riches is made the source of all sin. Brunhilde is the intermediary through whose sacrifices, forced and voluntary, heaven and earth are joined by the bond of love, by which it is destined the world shall finally be redeemed.

The first scene to which we are introduced in the "Gotterdammerung" is one of marked weirdness, showing three Norns, or goddesses of fate, sitting on those rocky heights where the Valkyries were wont to assemble, weaving a web of destiny. They are forbidding creatures, wrapped in long black robes, winding a golden thread, and recounting the rape of the Rhinegold and the adventures of Siegfried. They sing also of the time when Wotan fashioned an invincible spear from the limb of an ash tree, and how he left an eye in pledge at the mystic well to obtain therefrom a draught of wisdom. Sorrowfully, the third Norn, in dirge-like recitation, continues the tale of her sisters by telling how, on an evil day, Wotan returned with his shivered spear and commanded the gods to hew down the ash tree and to pile its limbs about Walhalla's Palace that the giants had built, since which act he has been sitting in moody silence before the castle, awaiting the fiery doom that Erda predicted should befall the gods. While thus reciting, the Norns unconsciously draw the thread so tightly that it snaps, whereupon with suddenness they vanish into a gloomy cavern of the earth, to join their mother, Erda.

The next action begins with a view of Valkyrie's rock, the same as at the conclusion of "Siegfried." The time is night, but day soon breaks upon the mountain, and as the roseate glow of morning lights up the peak and discloses the valley, Siegfried, full panoplied, comes out of the cave, followed by Brunhilde, who leads her horse, "Grani." Brunhilde bids her hero a tender farewell in a touching song, "Did I not send thee," bidding him go forth for performance of the duties which destiny has marked out for him, leaving her meantime in the fire-encircled sanctuary, where she will anxiously bide his return. Siegfried, sorrowful, but bound by duty, before taking his departure, places upon her finger the magic ring gained from the dragon, adjuring her to carefully keep it as a pledge of their troth, until his coming, and she in turn presents him with her good steed "Grani." All the preceding is but a prelude to the first act, and when the curtain rises again it is to show the Hall of the Gibichungs, on the Rhine, with Gunther and his sister, Gutrune, upon a throne, and Hagen, their half-brother, seated in front of them.

Hagen is one of the despised breed of Gibichs, distinguished for his deceit and cunning, who has been begotten by Alberich to assist the dwarf's ambition to recover the magic ring. When the curtain rises, the three are discovered considering a question of marriage whereby to strengthen the Gibich race. Hagen urges Gunther to seek a wife, and suggests that the beautiful Brunhilde is one most suitable to his station. Gunther receives the proposal with manifest favor, but both he and Gutrune eagerly inquire how she, hedged by a wall of flames, which only Siegfried has the courage to pass, may be reached and won.

The wily creature of personified deceit, to whom, as a Nibelung, the future is revealed, answers Gunther by telling him that Siegfried is now on his way hither, whose coming may advance their measures; and proposes to compound a potion, a draught of which will compel forgetfulness of present love and obligation, under which unholy influence Siegfried can be made to conceive a burning passion for Gutrune, and to perform any heroic act commanded whereby to win her hand. Scarcely has Hagen announced his proposal when Siegfried's horn is heard, followed by his appearance, crossing the river in a boat. Upon landing he is heartily welcomed by Gunther, who conducts him to the ancestral hall of the Gibichungs, while Hagen leads his horse away and cares for him, but quickly returns again. Gutrun looks wistfully upon the hero, of whom she has heard so much, but at his approach she retires, in visible confusion, wounded by love's arrow.

Gunther receives Siegfried with much flattery, and to show his hospitality offers to bestow upon him all the soil, serfs and possessions of his birthright, which Siegfried disdains to accept, since by his strong limbs and good sword Needful he may gain what pleases him. Hagen, standing behind the two, ventures to remark that it has been told Siegfried is lord and keeper of the Nibelheim hoard of treasure, which Siegfried answers:

> "This wealth I did well-nigh forget,
> For so worthless do I deem the gold,
> That within a cavern have I left it,
> Where once a dragon long kept guard,
> Retaining only this network which I cannot use."

Hagen immediately perceives that the steel network, which Siegfried esteems so little, is the tarnhelm, and explains its wondrous properties to turn to any shape, at will, whoso wears it, or to whirl upon the instant to any land, however distant, the lucky possessor. Having so explained, Hagen asks if he bore away any other part of the treasure? to which Siegfried replies that a ring he kept, until he gave it to a sweet woman, worthy to wear it as a troth.

Hagen pushes open the door to Gutrune's room and summoning her, she enters bearing a drinking horn, which with words of welcome she proffers Siegfried, and presses him to quench his thirst. Bowing low, Siegfried takes the horn and drinks to the memory of Brunhilde, his bride. The love-potion mixed in the wine shows its swift effect, for scarcely is the horn emptied when Siegfried flames with passion for Gutrune, thus revealing:

> "Ha! sweetest maid! Screen those bright beams!
> The heart in my breast burns with their strength;
> In fiery streams I feel my blood boiling in my veins.
> Gunther, what name hath thy sister?"

When told that she is called Gutrune, Siegfried seizes her hand and with impatient ardor he declares his love, until in diffidence, and with feelings of unworthiness she disengages herself from his embraces and retires from the room. Siegfried now turns to Gunther and eagerly asks if he has a wife, to which the latter makes answer that no woman has yet been wooed, nor wife he scarce can win, for the one upon whom his heart is fixed liveth upon a far-off rock, begirt by flames, which he may not approach, though "he who the fire can brave, is Brunhilde's fitting mate." Siegfried repeats softly, as if striving to recall a faded memory, "A far-off rock's

DIE GOTTERDAMMERUNG

her home, a fire doth breast her hall!" but the glimpse is only momentary, a fleeting vision that produces no real impression, and through his now unquenchable infatuation for Gutrune he offers to serve Gunther:

> "I fear not the fire, thy bride I will fetch;
> For thy own am I, and my arm is thine;
> If Gutrune for wife I may gain,
> Brunhilde I will bring thee!"

Gunther is pleased with the proposal, but marvels how it may be accomplished, not conceiving how Brunhilde can be deceived. Gleefully Siegfried dissipates Gunther's fears, by telling him that by aid of the tarnhelm he his form may assume and thereby safely pass the fire, which will pale before his advance. The stratagem is hailed with such satisfaction that Gunther suggests that a bond of brotherhood be established between them, which is performed by pricking their arms with a sword-point and mingling their blood in wine drunk from the same cup. Having by this ceremony taken an inviolate oath, the two enter Siegfried's boat and hasten away upon their quest, leaving Hagen to watch and guard Gibich Hall. As the two float down the stream Hagen congratulates himself on the pleasing prospect of recovering the ring, which he doubts not Siegfried, in Gunther's form, will bring back and give as a reward for Gutrune.

After a brief orchestral interlude, a second curtain is withdrawn showing the Valkyrie's rock, and Brunhilde seated in front of a cave, gazing tenderly upon the ring, and often kissing it for the pledge it sealed between her and Siegfried. Suddenly her thoughts are disturbed by a visit from Waltraute, a sister Valkyrie, who gaining Brunhilde's attention, informs her that since with shattered spear Wotan returned to Walhalla he has set before the palace in deepest dejection, resolved that when the doom shall fall, overwhelming the gods, Walhalla shall be his funeral pyre. But Waltraute confesses that she has often heard his wailings, and his predictions that if the Rhine daughters should regain the ring they would avert the curse that Alberich laid upon the gods, and save Walhalla from Erda's predicted doom. Brunhilde remains unmoved throughout this recital, as if indifferent to the fate that has been recounted, until Waltraute reminds her that she being bearer of the ring should restore it to the Rhine maidens, since such a sacrifice will serve to save her father and all the gods from destruction. Brunhilde is weaned from heaven by the great love she holds for Siegfried, a love that has taught her the secret of real happiness, and she answers her sister:

> "One look at this dear ring, one glitter of its bright gold,
> Are more to me than the eternal happiness of all the gods."

Sorrowful in her disappointment, Waltraute leaves Brunhilde, and as she disappears a horn is heard sounding in the valley, which Brunhilde recognizes as that of Siegfried's, and joyfully she hurries to give him a happy wife's welcome. Flames are seen to dart up over the cliff, out of which Siegfried appears to rise, but it is Siegfried in Gunther's form, wearing the tarnhelm, which, like a visor, covers his face. As this vision of a stranger comes fairly into view, Brunhilde retreats in consternation, crying, "Betrayed! What man art thou?" Siegfried pauses, and leaning upon his shield, in altered and deeper voice exclaims:

"A Gibichung am I, and Gunther it is who, maid, will mate with thee." In wildest grief Brunhilde accuses Wotan of perpetrating this other shame, to persecute her to the very deeps of humiliation and woe. Siegfried, unrelenting in his purpose, with mind diverted by the magic potion that has made him slave to a lawless love and faithless to his faithful spouse, leaps from the rock and making bold to obtrude in his disguise upon the terrified woman, demands that she consent to marriage. To preserve herself from what she regards as threatened violence, Brunhilde points her finger, on which is Siegfried's ring, exclaiming:

> "Stand back! bow to this token!
> No shame can touch me from thee
> While yet this ring is my shield!
> Stronger than steel makes me the ring;
> And none may rend it from me."

This declaration excites Siegfried to anger, who fiercely rushes upon Brunhilde. She eludes him at first and runs rapidly, but Siegfried pursues, and seizing her at last, after a long struggle he succeeds in wrenching the ring from her finger, while she, half fainting, is driven before him into the cave. But mindful of his oath, to wed by proxy, Siegfried draws his sword and with an earnest avowal makes it a witness to the chastity of his wooing, with which powerful scene the curtain falls upon the first act.

Act II begins with a scene of great beauty, showing the Rhine bank, before the ancestral hall of the Gibichungs. The shore rises towards a rocky slope, checkered with mountain paths, on which are to be seen three altar stones, dedicated respectively to Fricka, Wotan, and Donner. The time is night, and Hagen, with spear and shield, is discovered by a flood of moonlight, asleep in the hall, with Alberich crouching in front leaning his arms on Hagen's knees. The latter is aroused by Alberich's request to know if he has conceived some fresh artifice to secure the ring. Hagen assures him that it soon shall be theirs: "The ring I'll lay hands on;—happily rest. My soul swears it, therefore cease from thy sorrow." Reposing confidence in the oath and cunning of his son, Alberich disappears, leaving Hagen alone. The sun rises, mirroring its face in the dimpled waters of the Rhine, upon which Hagen gazes with fixed eyes, until suddenly Siegfried appears in his own form, but still wearing the tarnhelm. He accosts the drowsy Hagen and tells him that he is just returned from Brunhilde's rock, but being speedy in his travels, he has far outstripped the maid and Gunther, who follow in a boat, and will arrive presently. Hagen now calls Gutrune to come forth and greet Siegfried, who hath mastered Brunhilde. Upon her appearance Siegfried sings, "Now make me welcome, Gibich maid," in which he exultantly recounts his adventures in gaining Brunhilde as a bride for Gunther.

When Siegfried has concluded his story, and retired with Gutrune, Hagen goes out upon a height overlooking the Rhine, and there blows a loud blast on a great cattle horn, which is answered by other horns in many directions, until soon from the mountains and valleys armed vassals rush onto the stage. These come inquiring the cause of their summons, to which Hagen answers that it is to give a fitting reception to Gunther, who is bringing home a wife. He thereupon orders that sacrifices be offered to the gods: a bull to Wotan, a boar to Froh, a sheep to Fricka, and a he-goat to Donner. When all has been prepared, Gunther and Brunhilde arrive in a boat, which is dragged ashore by willing hands, while other vassals shout and clash their weapons. While Brunhilde is being conducted up the slope by Gunther, he praises her beauty and promises that the Gibich race shall through her rise to high renown. Proceeding, the two pass on until they reach the hall, where Gunther pauses as Siegfried and Gutrune advance, attended by a train of women. Gunther congratulates Siegfried upon the happy fortune of his venture, which has united Brunhilde with

Gunther, and Gutrune with Siegfried. Brunhilde has shown no interest in the ceremonies of welcome, but dejectedly, with downcast eyes, she follows her master, until hearing the name Siegfried pronounced she startles, and dropping Gunther's hand she moves one pace towards Siegfried, then recoils in horror, at which the company wonder at her action, fearing that she has become distraught. Siegfried steps nearer and attempts to soothe her fears, at which Brunhilde, almost fainting, appeals to know why he is thus associated with Gutrune? Siegfried, laid under a ban of confusion by the magic potion that has destroyed remembrance of past events, innocently tells her that Gutrune is his wife, as she herself is wife to Gunther, which pronouncement fires Brunhilde with such indignation that in broken accents she exclaims, "I? . . . Gunther? . . . You lie!" Then, overcome by the violence of her feelings, she is about to fall, but is caught in Siegfried's arms, uttering, softly and faintly, "Siegfried . . . knows me not?" Siegfried calls to Gunther, that his wife is fainting, and pointing to him tries to arouse her by saying, "There stands your husband." As his hand is lifted, Brunhilde discovers the ring on Siegfried's finger, when with fearful impetuosity she launches her fury:

"On thy hand there I behold a ring!
Thou hold'st it wrongly.
It was ravished by this man (pointing to Gunther)
Tell me, by what means didst thou gain the ring?"

Siegfried attentively inspects the ring upon his finger, and struggles with his memory to recall how he came possessed of it, but he is able to remember nothing more than that the ring was not obtained from Gunther, and he so declares. Brunhilde, still vehement, charges Gunther with having torn it from her finger, to make it a marriage pledge, and exhorts him now to wrest it back again. In greatest perplexity he vows that he gave Siegfried nothing, whereupon Brunhilde, in frantic outburst prefers her accusation: "Ha! then, this one it was who wrenched the ring! Siegfried, the treacherous thief!" Siegfried is quite absorbed in contemplating the ring, and presently the cloud of forgetfulness that has overshadowed his mind partially uplifts, and he answers

"No girl, I ween, gave me this ring
Nor woman 'twas from whom the prize I won
This hoop I bear as the battle prize,
When at Hate Cave I slew the dragon"

Hagen, the cunning, having provoked the strife by his magic potion, now comes between, and flattering Brunhilde by name of "Noble Dame," tells her that if the ring Gunther has gained, it by right must remain his still, and that Siegfried has won it by a trick, which the traitor should pay for straight. This charge of deceit, a shameful stratagem, moves Brunhilde to greatest anguish, and when the company ask her to explain, she recites the story of her grief and provocation and entreats that her wrongs be revenged:

"Here let Brunhilde's heart straight be broken,
If he who wronged her may but be wrecked."

Gunther tries to calm her, but her wrath is loosed against him also, whom she bids begone as traitor too, and pointing to Siegfried, she cries out, "To him it was that I was wed!" With wide astonishment at such a claim, which he is unable to understand, he pronounces Brunhilde's words untrue, to disprove which he appeals to the proofs of blood-brotherhood made between Gunther and himself, and to his sword Needful, which guarded the oath intact, and by its keen edge kept him "sundered from this ill-omened bride." Brunhilde, stung to fury by Siegfried's plea, calls him lord of deceit, whose sword doth serve no proof, for though its blade is keen, known also to her is its scabbard, which reposed upon the wall, evidence of a "trusty friend, when a true love its master did win."

Siegfried, hoping to end the dispute, offers to submit the proof of his unsullied honor to the trial by spear, and obtains such weapon from Hagen for the ceremony. The vassals now form a circle around Siegfried and Hagen, and as the latter stretches forth his spear Siegfried lays two fingers upon its point and repeats an oath pledging himself to truth, and calling down a vengeance upon his head "if Brunhilde is really wronged —if I have injured my friend."

When the oath is taken Brunhilde forces her way into the circle, and thrusting Siegfried's fingers away from the spear, which she believes he has profaned, lays her own fingers upon its tip and utters:

> Haft of war, hallowed weapon,
> Hold thou my oath from dishonor!
> Spear point, aid thou my speech!
> I sanctify thy strength to his destruction!
> And I bless thy blade, withal,
> That it may blight him,
> For broken are all his oaths,
> And perjurer now doth he prove!"

"When I sought to serve my spring,
the pride inspired my aid"

The vassals, in greatest commotion, appeal to Donner, the god of tempest, to silence this terrible shame. Siegfried tries to still the tumult, by bidding Gunther give no heed to the woman's lies, and to leave her alone for a while until her mind disturbance slackens, which by some demon's spite has been drawn upon them all. Going close to Gunther, that others may not hear his words, Siegfried expresses fear that the tarnhelm may have served him a trick, but bids him take courage, for a woman's ire is soon expended, and Brunhilde will one day be thankful for having gained so good a husband. Then, to the company, Siegfried invites them to the marriage feast, that has too long been kept waiting, and placing his arm about Gutrune, leads the way to the banquet hall, followed by all save Hagen, Brunhilde and Gunther. A silence succeeds, which is broken by Brunhilde marveling what infernal craft, or magician's rod, has wrought this woe, by which she has become booty of a master who may so lightly give her away, and asks, "Whose sword shall I have to beg, with which I may sever my bonds?" Hagen perceives that his opportunity has arrived, and with show of valor he offers to avenge her wrongs, even to the slaying of Siegfried, if it be her wish. Brunhilde laughs bitterly at his proposal, admonishing that, in the hour of loving confidence,

she has made him invulnerable to all weapons, save alone in his back, which needed no spell of protection, for Siegfried never turned his front from mortal foe. Hagen rises quickly, exclaiming, "And there he shall be speared!" which pleases Brunhilde, but Gunther hesitates to approve a crime that will leave his sister widowed. His compunction, however, is overcome by Brunhilde charging him with being a timid spouse, and treacherous friend, hidden behind a hero, whose faint heart ill becomes a lordly race. The conspiracy is finally concluded, and agreement is made that Gutrune shall be told, when the murderous deed is done, that Siegfried has been killed by a wild boar which he had wounded and driven to bay in the rocky fastnesses. This infamous compact to conceal the crime having been made, Gunther and Brunhilde turn hastily toward the hall, at the entrance to which they are met by Siegfried and Gutrune, he wearing a wreath of oak leaves, and she garlanded with flowers, which scene affords an effective climax for the second act.

"Perhaps they found it one 1"

Act III.—The closing act of "Die Gotterdammerung" opens with a scene which represents a wild, rocky shore of the Rhine, in the waters of which Woglinda, Wellgunda, and Flosshilde, guardian nymphs of the Rhinegold, are disporting. They soon rise to the surface and sing an exhortation to the sun-god to send a hero who will regain for them the gold stolen by Alberich. Their song is hushed at the sound of Siegfried's horn, and they disappear under the water as the hero appears upon the cliff, complaining that he has lost the track of a bear which he has been hotly pursuing. The nymphs rise again and promise to help him find the game if he will give them the ring. He regards it as of no more value than a trinket won by battle with a dragon, but thinks even such reward is too much to pay for sight of a sorry bear, besides, to give it would vex his wife, who prizes it more than he. The nymphs accuse him of suffering a wife to rule, but he is unmoved by their banter, and, disappointed, the three dive out of sight, pronouncing him a miserly fellow. Siegfried remains quiet for a while, but hearing no sound, and finding no signs of the bear, he descends to the water's edge and calls the nymphs, promising to give them the ring. They promptly rise to the surface, but instead of beseeching, they tell him that if he keep the ring it will bring a curse. He replaces the ring upon his finger, and bids them describe the evil which they predict, whereupon the nymphs explain that the ring was wrought from gold which in the Rhine once glowed; that he who shaped it with labor and lost it in shame, laid a curse upon it by which all who possess it shall be slain; that as the dragon perished by his sword, so will this very day fall a victim unless he giveth up the ring, that it may be hidden in the Rhine, which alone can break the spell. This threatened calamity decides Siegfried to keep the ring, for as he has never learned to fear, and holds the great sword Needful, he will defy the fate which they have predicted. The Rhine maidens thereupon call him a dullard, and declaring that a stately woman will this day inherit the ring, they swim away.

As the nymphs disappear calls of hunting horns are heard on the hills, which Siegfried answers by loud blasts upon his own. Gunther, Hagen and many vassals descend the heights, who finding Siegfried ask him to join them in refreshments. Game is stacked, skins of wine are produced, and all seat themselves, but Siegfried has been unsuccessful in the hunt, and therefore requests that he may have food from their bags and drink from their skins, which Hagen and Gunther are willing to give, but they banter him on his luckless pursuit. He tells them that had he reckoned rightly three wild young water maids he might have won this morning, who sang in the Rhine their warning that ere the wane of day he should die. Hagen, with sinister look, observes. "A dismal chase were that if the hunter, luckless still, by lurking beasts were laid low." Siegfried seats himself between Hagen and Gunther, and vassals fill drinking horns with wine which they offer, but as Siegfried drinks, and passes the horn to Gunther the latter professes to see only blood in the cup, which Siegfried proposes shall

Messenger Announcing the Death of Siegfried

DIE GOTTERDAMMERUNG.

be the mixture that seals their brotherhood. They ask him about the report they have heard of his ability to understand the birds, whereupon, wishing to entertain his visitors, he repeats the story of his adventures. In this song, with his orchestral accompaniments, are all the motives heard in the Siegfried division of the "Nibelungen." It is a wonderful medley and blending of the sword melody, the tempest in the wood, voice of the wood-pecker, Mime's enticement, lapping of flames, and Brunhilde's awakening, composing a musical description which may well be called marvelous.

Hagen secretly pours into Siegfried's horn an antidote to the potion that steeped his mind in forgetfulness, and then requests him to describe his quest and wakening of Brunhilde. Upon the instant he remembers all, and tells the story of how he was guided by a bird to the flame-encircled bed whereon Brunhilde slept, and how he kissed sleep from her long-closed eyes, and won her for bride, most beautiful of women.

As Siegfried's descriptive song concludes, two messengers of evil, in the form of ravens, flap lazily across the stage, and the curse motive, in gloomy grandeur, solemnly stately, pours forth from the orchestra. At sight of these birds of ill omen, Siegfried starts up quickly, and looking after them turns his back to Hagen, who seizing the opportunity, casts his spear into the hero's back. Gunther and the vassals appear horrified, crying: "Hagen, what deed is this!" Siegfried swings his shield aloft to crush Hagen, but his strength has failed, and he falls upon it. Hagen, pointing at the prostrate form, pronounces his deed an act of retribution, and then turning away, disappears over the hills. Gunther is seized with anguish at the cowardly crime, though he had abetted it, and the vassals express their sympathy. Siegfried moves slightly, and opening his eyes he gives utterance to the ramblings of his mind, to describe his vision of Brunhilde, of her beauteous form, enchanting charms, and odorous breath, and with the words, "Brunhilde beckons to me!" he expires.

HAGEN THROWING THE MYSTIC TREASURE INTO THE RHINE

Night has now thrown down her shrouds. The vassals place Siegfried's body on his shield and bear it away in mournful procession. As the bearers pass, the moon breaks through a cloud and illumines the funeral train, followed by mists that rise from the Rhine until they obscure the stage, permitting a change of scene without dropping the curtain. The Siegfried funeral march, which is composed chiefly of the motives of Siegmund, the love duet between Siegmund and Sieglinda, the sword and the Walsung action, and Siegfried's theme, all interwoven in fortissimo and crescendo effects, is the highest delineation of musical expression, eminently fitting as a lamentation dirge for a demigod.

The next scene is the hall of the Gibichungs, a magnificently beautiful setting, framed in moonlight that falls upon the castle and shimmers in the Rhine waters. Gutrune enters from her chamber, thinking she has heard Siegfried's horn, and expresses anxiety for his return. As she is about to re-enter her room she hears Hagen's voice without, and pauses, transfixed with fear, as if some premonition advised her of a great calamity Hagen comes shouting, "Wake up! wake up! Torches and firebrands here! Fair booty bring we along." Entering the hall he bids Gutrune greet the stalwart hero, Siegfried, who is coming home. Behind him are men and women with torches, followed by the train carrying Siegfried's body, with

Gunther among them. Gutrune, betraying her terror, expresses astonishment that she has not heard Siegfried's horn, at which the wicked Hagen tells her the bloodless hero will blow it no more, neither in the chase nor battle, for "a wild boar's ill-fated victim: Siegfried, 'tis thy husband's corpse." As the bearers enter with the body, Gutrune flings herself upon it in a paroxysm of grief and despair. She will not believe Siegfried has been slain by a boar, but suspecting assassination she accuses Gunther of the murder, until Hagen boastfully confesses that it was his own hand that slew him, and now he claims the ring. Gunther steps forward to prevent Hagen from gaining the coveted treasure, but the curse is not yet completed, for Hagen strikes him dead, then is about to snatch the ring from Siegfried's finger when, behold! the dead man lifts his arm menacingly, at which Hagen starts back aghast and the women scream with fright. Brunhilde now comes upon the scene, at sight of whom Gutrune is inflamed with anger and accuses her of provoking Siegfried's murder. Brunhilde answers that she alone is the hero's lawful wife, whose love she would have retained had not Gutrune won him by the iniquitous ruse of a magic draught. The truth thus proclaimed, in the presence of two great tragedies, compels Gutrune's acknowledgment that she is victim of a treachery which she has herself been accessory to, and thereupon takes her position as mourner over Gunther's body. Brunhilde, calm, deliberate, in her agony, now steps forward, and in solemn words declares she has come to avenge the death of her lord. Hagen stands leaning defiantly upon his spear and shield, sunk in gloomy meditation. After gazing for a while upon Siegfried's body, struggling with her despair, Brunhilde turns towards the people, and with solemn utterance, that reflects her affliction, she bids them:

> "Friends, let fitting funeral pyre
> Be reared by the river here,
> Hot and high kindle the flames
> To consume him who was hero o'er all!
> His steed bring to me here,
> To its master straight it shall bear me;
> For my body burneth to share in the honor
> That here we show unto him."

Obedient to Brunhilde's will a great funeral pyre is raised before the Hall, which, when finished, the women adorn with drapery, and flowers, and Siegfried's body is laid thereon. As the immolation is being prepared for, Brunhilde gazes earnestly upon the dead face of her falsely-true lover-husband, and sorrowfully exclaims:

> "What sunny light outstreams from his look!
> The very truest was he, yet could betray!"

And pays to him the tribute of a devotion which loyal wife alone can feel, whose heart is rended by disclosure that his fealty was steadfast till brought to violation by influence which the arts of hellish covetousness inspired, and which the gods made possible to prevail. To these gods, however, she addresses her petition, beseeching that they hear her wild lament, and save the soul of Siegfried from the curse that Wotan has pronounced.

While Brunhilde is thus voicing her lamentations, at her signal the men take up the body of Siegfried and place it upon the funeral pyre, and when it is so disposed she draws the ring of evil inspiration from his finger and places it upon her own, but suddenly she reflects that this golden circlet, which might have been pledge of marriage, has been in fact the cause of woe unutterable to both gods and men, and she calls the nymphs to

THE HAND OF DEAD SIEGFRIED RISES THREATENINGLY EXPOSING THE RING

claim it as their own when it has been purified by the fire which shall now consume Siegfried and her own body. Then snatching a torch from a vassal she thrusts it into the pile, which quickly bursts into flames. While the fire is raging Brunhilde bids the two wailing ravens fly to her fire-girt rock and bear to Loki command to transfer the flames to Walhalla, that the heavens of the gods may be destroyed, saying: "I leave my treasure of knowledge to the world. All the splendors that earth offers, may not be compared to love, which is the incomparable."

— Grani, my horse, greet thee again!
Wouldst thou know what journey we follow?
By fire illumined lies there thy lord
Siegfried, the star of my life
To meet with thy master neighest thou merrily?
Lo! how the flame doth leap and allure thee!
Feel how my breast too hotly doth burn
Sparkling fireflame my spirit enfolds
Oh, but to clasp him, recline in his arms!
In maddening emotion once more to be his!
Heiajaho! Grani! Greet we our hero!
Siegfried! Siegfried! see!
Sweetly greets thee thy wife!

At Brunhilde's request Grani is brought, upon whose back she mounts, and with a last farewell she rides into the flames, which now spread so rapidly as to threaten Gibich Hall. At this fearsome sight the women cower in abject terror as if helpless to avert a fiery fate, but suddenly some strange power appears to intervene, the pillars fall into smoking ruins, and there arise clouds of smoke that form a pall on the horizon. The cause of this expiration of the flames is soon discovered, for the rapidly swelling Rhine pours a flood over the fire, upon the rushing surface of which are the Rhine daughters swimming close to the smouldering embers, and calling for the ring. Hagen, who has watched Brunhilde with increasing anxiety, is much alarmed by the appearance and cries of the three nymphs, and in a frenzy of anger at the prospect of losing the mystic ring he leaps into the stream to contest possession of the treasure, but Woglinda and Wellgunda drag him under the waves, while Flosshilde triumphantly holds the ring aloft. In the northern sky a great glow is discovered; it is from the fire that has seized Walhalla, at which the company gaze in consternation as the curtain falls upon the last act.

THE RHINE NYMPHS REGAIN THE RING AND DRAG HAGEN BENEATH THE WAVES

FRIEDRICH VON FLOTOW.

FLOTOW, who was born April 27, 1812, had the excellent fortune to be son of a wealthy and influential tradesman of Rentendorf, in the duchy of Mecklenberg-Schwerin, whose ambition was to make a diplomat of him, but met so many discouragements, through the erratic disposition of Friedrich, that the design to fit him for a diplomatic career was presently abandoned. Subsequent events, however, proved that the young man was of better material than his early conduct indicated, for being thrown into association with artists and highly educated persons, his latent talent for musical composition was aroused, which he developed by a course of study at the Paris Conservatory, where he became a pupil of Reicha. At the outbreak of the July revolution of 1830, the greatly disturbed condition of affairs in Paris rendering it unsafe for foreigners to remain in the city, Flotow returned to his native city, but two years later he went again to Paris and industriously renewed his studies. In 1836 his first composition, "Pierre et Catherine," was produced at the small Theatre de l'Hotel de Castellane, and in the same year his second lyrical essay was given at the Chateau de Royaumont.

While the success of these two efforts was far from great, Flotow found enough encouragement to produce other compositions, but his work was marked by such care, and he proceeded with so much caution, being keenly sensitive to criticism, that his creations were submitted at long intervals, for which reason he failed to achieve any considerable reputation until the public representation of his "Wreck of the Medusa," in 1839. This splendid work was first performed at the Theatre de la Renaissance, where it had fifty-four representations, but Flotow was so dissatisfied with the lyrical construction that in 1845 he rewrote the score and entitled it "Die Matrosen" (The Sailors), which was given in Hamburg, though with even less favor than was accorded the original work.

In 1848 Paris was torn by another revolution, from the terrors of which Flotow escaped by fleeing to Mecklenberg, where he remained for a period of fifteen years, devoting his energies all the while to composition. In 1850 he was honored by the Grand Duke of Mecklenberg, who appointed him Intendant of Court Music at Schwerin, an office which was more honorable than active, engaging so little of his time that his serious work remained uninterrupted.

It is a singular thing, worthy to be noted, that after his appointment as Intendant of Court Music, Flotow, from a high estate as a really great composer, fell to a place of mediocrity, from which, though he made many efforts, he was never able to rise. Indeed, his power began to wane markedly from the time that he left Paris in 1848, after which he never produced anything comparable with his earlier compositions. When he took the position of chief musician at the theatre of the Grand Duke of Mecklenberg, though there was a small salary connected with the position, Flotow entered upon his duties with great energy, stimulated by an ambition to exercise a strong influence upon German music, which seemed to furnish a means to win the fame which he thirsted for. His success for the first three years equaled his hopes, but thereafter he fell under suspicion as an intriguer, and was so harassed by jealous rivals, as well as by members of the court, that in 1863 he resigned what had become a hateful position and returned to Paris.

After his third return to the French capital Flotow turned his attention largely to chamber music, with some success, but in 1866 he essayed comic opera again, producing "Zelda," which was given a splendid representation at the Opera Comique that year, but like many others of his compositions, it proved to be a failure, which so disgusted him, esteeming, as authors are apt to do, that public disfavor was due to prejudice and ignorant inappreciation, that in 1868 he moved to Vienna intending to make that city his permanent abode.

It is interesting, as it is instructive, to consider how many operas Flotow composed, and how small is his reputation, if we deduct that which he achieved by "Martha" and "Alessandro Stradella," which may be called productions of his youth. Is it that the Pierian spring ran dry ere he could quench his thirst? or that Melopœia dashed the cup from his grasp when only his lips were wetted? And yet so wonderful are the very few compositions upon which his fame is based that as a creator of comic opera no one may be placed above him.

The works with which Flotow is credited, besides those already mentioned, are as follows: "Seraphina" (1836); "The Miners" and "Rob Roy" (1839); "The Duchess of Guise" (1840); "The Forester" (1647); "L'ame en Peine" [A Troubled Conscience], (1847); "The Grand Duchess" (1850); "Indra" (1853); "Riga" (1855); "Rubezahl" (1854); "Hilda" (1855); "Albin" (1856); "The Miller of Meran" (1856); "Widow Grapin," operette (1859); "Pianelle" (1860); "Wintermarch" (1862); "Die Libelle," ballet (1866); "Tanakonig," ballet (1867); "Runenstein" (1868); "The Phantom" (1869); "Naida" (1873); "The Flower of Harlem" (1876); "The Enchantress" (1878).

Besides this formidable list are several compositions which were produced after Flotow's death, but even his fame and the posthumous admiration which is usually greatest, failed to give them popularity. Of the many here noticed, only "The Phantom" justified the hazard of many repetitions. This opera was given with some success in France, Germany and England, but it was short-lived, and has not been heard for many years, nor is its revival probable.

An interesting episode in Flotow's career occurred in 1838, at the initial performance of his three act opera, "The Duchess of Guise," at the Renaissance Theatre, Paris. Upon this occasion, ever memorable, the first ladies of Louis Philippe's court condescended to appear not only as patrons but as performers. In 1830 the Poles, incited thereto by promise of help from France, rebelled against their harsh Russian oppressors, and an attempt was made to seize the Grand Duke Constantine at his residence near Warsaw. This really hopeless uprising caused untold misery. The insurgents were first led by Chlopicki, but afterwards the command devolved on Prince Adam Czartoryski, who fought valiantly but against great odds, and in the latter part of 1831 was vanquished with the loss of more than half his followers. Such suffering was entailed by this untimely revolution, and French sympathy was so strong for the subjugated Poles, that the Princess Czartoryski, an exile in Paris, arranged a performance for the benefit of her countrymen. In the opera, "The Duchess of Guise," Mme. de Lagrange made her debut, and the chorus parts were filled by duchesses and princesses of the Faubourg St. Germain, upon whose persons it is declared diamonds to the value of more than two millions of dollars shone. This was the greatest day in Flotow's life, gauged by the demonstrations with which his name was hailed, and the magnificence that attended the presentation of his composition, but grand as was the occasion, glamoured by fine jewels and the unusual spectacle of royal dames doing chorus duty before the footlights, the opera was successful only this single night.

During his career from 1836 until his death at Darmstadt, January 24, 1883, Flotow composed thirty-four pieces, operas, ballets, operettas, besides many overtures, songs and chamber music. His operas are singularly melodious, and though Italian in character, are thoroughly original, well deserving the reputation that is generally given him of being probably the most popular creator of comic opera that Germany has produced, occupying a place in advance of even Lortzing and Kreutzer. His fame, however, was chiefly obtained, and rests most securely upon "Martha," which had its initial representation in Vienna, November 25, 1847; and upon "Stradella," first produced in Hamburg, December 30, 1844. These operas have found unqualified and equal favor in all civilized countries, the former especially, its deliciously sweet airs being as familiar to the rustic as to the opera patron, for they are sung and played everywhere. The most brilliant jewel of song in "Martha" is "The Last Rose of Summer," one of dear Tom Moore's masterpieces of verse, to which Flotow gave a musical setting that is as softly ruthful and tenderly plaintive as are the sentiments of the poem, and which with "Home, Sweet Home," will survive as long as the human heart appreciates and is responsive to sympathy and love.

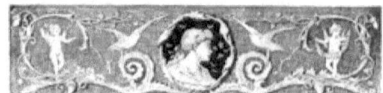

Stradella

(AFTER THE ORIGINAL PAINTING BY ADOLFO HOHENSTEIN)

STRADELLA—" *When repenting, in lamenting*
They before thee bend their knee;
And by deeds of expiation
Do their guilt to thee confess."

ACT III.—LAST SCENE

STRADELLA.

By Friedrich Von Flotow.

STRADELLA is a charming romantic opera in three acts, which, like wine, seems to grow better with age. Though rarely heard in America it is frequently sung in all the European capitals, where it has long remained a pronounced favorite. Stradella was first produced as a lyric drama in 1837, at the Palais Royal Theatre, Paris, where it scored a distinct triumph. This high appreciation was shortlived, however, due to weaknesses in the libretto which the sparkling, piquant, stirring and often fervid music could not relieve, an illustration of the necessity that words and score shall be of equal excellence. The defects complained of were corrected, in a measure, by rewriting the libretto, by changing several of the situations, and also by making improvements in the score, in which new form the opera was given in Hamburg, December 30, 1844, and has kept the boards in undiminished popularity ever since. "Stradella" received its English baptism in London, 1846, but the version, by Bunn, showed considerable departure from the original, not entirely to its benefit, though no one has attempted a better adaptation since. The opera is remarkably melodious, and the denouements are as delightful as they are happily conceived.

The libretto of "Allessandro Stradella" follows closely the historical story, as narrated by Bordelot and Boussel, except that the lovers, instead of being slain by hired assassins, as in the tale, are blissfully united in the conclusion, thus converting tragedy into a romantic comedy. The work is characterized by several exceedingly beautiful numbers, notably by the following: Stradella's charming serenade, "List, lady, list!" an exquisite nocturne, "Over hills, through valleys wending," a stirring carnival chorus, "High in air your voices lifting;" Leonora's fervid recitative, "Awake, my soul, to heaven its homage paying," the drinking song of Malvolio and Barbarino, "Nothing is half so good as wine from the wood;" a ballad by Stradella, "Deep in the valley, concealed from all eyes," a delightful terzetto, "Tell me now, friend Barbarino;" and Stradella's beautiful hymn, "Holy Virgin, grant consolation."

The story concerns the wooing of an Italian minstrel and singer named Stradella, a noble-appearing youth, and of generous sentiment. By song and pleadings he wins the heart of Leonora, the fair ward of Bassi, a wealthy patrician of Venice, who has himself conceived a passion for Leonora and by foul means, if necessary, would make her his wife. This purpose is defeated by the elopement of Stradella and Leonora to Rome, where they find refuge at the house of Campanani and are presently married, but not until they have had many adventures, which the lyric story describes. Bassi, angered to the point of desperation by the prompt measures of the lovers, hires two desperadoes, Malvolio and Barbarino, to pursue Stradella, and to kill him as quickly as opportunity will permit. Under this impious engagement, separately made, that neither of the assassins may know the designs of the other, the two proceed to Rome, where directly upon arriving they discover the house in which Stradella and Leonora have found a welcome to prepare for their wedding. When the bridal party start for the church to celebrate the nuptials Malvolio appears at the house, which to his surprise he finds is empty, but there are so many evidences of occupancy that he concludes the occupants are temporarily absent and will soon return. After entering and looking carefully about to assure himself that he is alone, Malvolio locks the door and draws from his pocket a paper, from which he reads the agreement he has made with Bassi binding himself to kill Stradella for a fixed reward. While Malvolio is thus refreshing his mind as to the provisions of the compact Barbarino approaches the house and attempts to gain admittance by the door. Getting no response to his knocks, and finding the door locked, he makes his way to an open window and climbs in. The noise of Barbarino's intrusion arouses Malvolio, who, having no doubt that it is a burglar, tries to expel him. The two draw their daggers and engage vigorously until their lopped hats are knocked off in the tussle and they recognize each other as old companions in many crimes.

STRADELLA

Malvolio and Barbarino are amused by their mistake and exchange assurances of concern for each other, and for their respective families, after which courtesies, each inquires of the other the motive of his presence in the house. An explanation of their mission follows, and surprise is expressed that they have both engaged, upon identical terms, to murder Stradella. A contention now ensues as to which shall perform the deed, but their differences are presently settled by an agreement to jointly execute the compact and to share the reward. Having so decided, the two leave the house to disguise themselves and await the coming of their victim.

When the marriage ceremony is performed, Stradella and his bride, accompanied by many friends, return to the house to celebrate the event. While the company are in the height of their festivities, Malvolio and Barbarino appear at the door in the disguise of pilgrims, and humbly crave shelter for the night, promising to contribute their help to the entertainment, if they may be permitted to do so. Stradella, hospitably inclined and unsuspecting their designs, welcomes the strangers with profuse generosity. During the merrymaking Stradella, by request, renders a ballad, which is so expressive, and so beautiful in its merciful sentiments, that Malvolio and Barbarino are persuaded to renounce their designs upon his life. They now become companionable, and being received as honored guests sing with Stradella and Leonora praises of their native land and the cities of their preference.

Decision of the two bravoes having been learned by Bassi, he seeks and upbraids them for their treachery and pusillanimity, but finding that threats are unavailing to move them from their merciful refusal to execute his designs. Bassi offers such increased rewards that he finally obtains from them a renewal of their promise to murder the minstrel lover. Having reason to believe that Stradella will soon return, Bassi, Malvolio and Barbarino conceal themselves behind a screen in the room, taking a position from which they may rush upon and dispatch their victim quickly with least fear of resistance or detection. Directly Stradella enters, who, unsuspicious of the presence of lurking enemies, rehearses a hymn to the Virgin which he is to sing in the church on the morrow. The conspirators stealthily approach him from behind and lift their daggers to strike him in the back, but their felt purpose is time and again suspended by the sweetness of the singer's voice and the merciful sentiments of his song, until at length, overcome by repentant feelings, they throw themselves at Stradella's feet, confessing the object of their ambush and imploring his forgiveness.

At the moment the three assassins are groveling for pardon, Leonora enters, startled to find her guardian in such a situation. Bassi, mortified by realization of his own baseness, now makes amends for the murderous design which his infatuation prompted, by giving his blessing to the united lovers, at which juncture pilgrims and populace enter to pay their homage to the married couple, whose happiness is made thus complete.

The opera opens with a chorus sung by Stradella's pupils, "While the moon is softly beaming," to which Stradella sings a response, of his ladylove, followed by an allegretto serenade:

"List, lady, list while love sings its fondest lay;
List to the words which echoeth far away."

After the serenade follows a charming nocturne that brings a response from Leonora:

"Behold! From an apartment yonder
There beams a glorious ray
Leonora, thy lover calleth,
Haste thee, waste not, let it away!"

STRADELLA.

Recognizing the voice of the serenader, Leonora appears upon the balcony, and begs Stradella to speak more softly, that spies may be near, with watchful eyes and bitter hate, to work their undoing. Stradella promises to protect her against all foes, but she, more mindful of the force that opposes her heart's desires, admonishes:

> "The minstrel's sem cannot avail
> 'Gainst one who holds both wealth and power;
> To-morrow doth my guardian cherish
> Belief that I his bride shall be
> But rather would I in the sea-bed lie,
> Than matched be for life with cruel Bassi."

Stradella beseeches her to flee with him, for though hirelings may guard each door, love explores all paths, nor halts at pending dangers. She is persuaded by his passionate pleadings, resolved that:

> "With thee, living, with thee, dying
> Is the constant thought of mine"

But as they are about to hasten away, sounds of a troop of masqueraders are heard, whereupon the lovers conceal themselves until the danger of discovery is past. A crowd of revelers soon appear, singing a jolly chorus praising Prince Carnival, and betraying evidence of having lingered at wayside wine shops. Stradella issues from his retreat believing he has nothing to fear from so gay a company, and giving them a cordial greeting, which is well received, he asks if they will lend him some needed assistance. They promise to be slaves to any of his proposals, whereupon he reveals his plight: that in a house near by lives one who claims his devotion, but that she has a guardian who nourishes an ambition to make her his own, wherefore she has prepared to fly. Securing the sympathy and promised help of the carnival maskers, Stradella repeats his serenade which brings forth Leonora from her hiding—and now follows one of the most exquisite numbers of the opera sung by Stradella, Leonora and the chorus.

While the company is singing, the voice of old Bassi is heard calling "Leonora! Leonora!" She is stricken with fear, but is reassured by the chorus, who make so much sport of Bassi that he shouts for the watch to help him find the runaway, to which the chorus warns the lovers, who are speeding away in a gondola:

> "Haste ye! haste ye! Let naught delay ye!
> The star of love your guide shall be.
> May all bliss now revive with thee.
> And the waves to bear ye on!"

Bassi continues his cries for help and the chorus to banter, until in his despair at losing her he offers a reward of one hundred scudi to any one who will find Leonora; but his appeals and bribes are alike scornfully refused, and Act I closes with the escape of Stradella and Leonora as the chorus resumes its laudation of Prince Carnival.

Act II begins with a recitative and air by Leonora. "Awake, my soul, to heaven homage paying," in which she expresses the joy that possesses her in realizing that she has escaped the thrall of Bassi, and found a home where golden hopes and coming joys rejoice her heart.

> Be witness to my fond heart's dreaming.
> Ye sun that floods the world with light,
> Ye flowers beneath his glory gleaming.
> Ye winds that flit not in their flight," etc.

When Leonora has concluded her song of triumphant love the chorus invites. "With devout but joyous feeling to the altar now repair," whereupon Stradella tells her the priest is ready and a happy company of friends, composing a bridal train, are waiting to witness their nuptials. Together they sing of plighted vows, now soon to be confirmed, in which the chorus joins, "Hark, the wedding bells are ringing," as all retire to

STRADELLA

seek the church. As the wedding party leaves the house Malvolio, who has been lurking near, comes upon the scene and approaching cautiously tries the door, which to his satisfaction he finds is unlocked, and that it opens to his touch. Entering, he looks carefully about to satisfy himself that no one is within, whereupon he recites the purpose of his visit, singing in gay measures to fortify his courage:

> "On the left bank of the Tiber,
> Near a hill that's radiant ever
> With flowers whose golden hues
> Cast a glorious lustre
> Over the house of Campanella.
> Where dwells the singer one Stradella.
> Ah, a minstrel greatest all do say,
> Who I promise shall become my prey."

Scarcely has Malvolio finished his congratulations over favoring opportunity, when Barbarino's voice is heard singing the same measures, thus betraying that he is upon an identical mission,—to kill Stradella. Finding the door to the Campanella residence locked, he enters by an open window, but is met by Malvolio, and a fight between the two desperadoes takes place, which ends abruptly by a mutual recognition. They laugh over their mistake, and inquire solicitously after each other's families, until Barbarino confesses that Bassi has hired him to perform a crime no less than the removal of Stradella. When asked to tell the terms of his compact, Barbarino repeats the instructions given him by Bassi, at which Malvolio is startled, for they are identical with the directions which he has himself received, differing not so much as a single word. It now becomes a question between them which one shall do the deed, but after some threatenings they agree to unite their fortunes, and executing the agreement which each has made with Bassi, divide the reward, whereupon they retire.

Stradella, Leonora and the chorus now enter, joyously singing of the happy event just transpired, of the sacred ties that have bound two hearts forevermore, and of promise to pay their devotions at the shrine of the Madonna on the morrow. While these felicitations are proceeding, Malvolio and Barbarino appear outside the house, where first listening to the carnival of joy within, they express gratification at finding matters so favorable for their designs, which they hope presently to execute with small fear of detection. They now go away to prepare their disguises as pilgrims, by which means to enter and gain the hospitality of the Campanella house. Stradella, in an ecstasy of happiness, bids the servants set the tables and bring wine his friends to welcome, as becomes one who has won the fairest of brides, and who must make his rapturous feelings manifest. While the company are drinking bumpers of wine and otherwise making merry in a celebration of the wedding, Malvolio and Barbarino enter the room in their pilgrim disguises, saying:

> "From distant country have we come,
> Stradella's minstrel fame to know;
> His voice we oft have heard it said
> Has pow'r to charm each list'ning ear."

Anticipating no evil intent behind this flattering speech, esteeming the world as rejoicing in his new found happiness, Stradella gives the two a cordial greeting and bestows his favors upon them with generous hand. He hastily bids the servants set the tables, to bring the best of wine and offer it in greatest plenty, that these new friends may receive a welcome as befits one who would provide good cheer for honored guests. Thereupon the chorus renders a drinking song:

> "When rich, red wine doth fill the glass,
> It moves the speeding hours to pass.
> The blood of grape, it thrills our hearts,
> And love and joy it thus imparts."

STRADELLA.

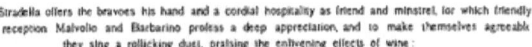

Stradella offers the bravoes his hand and a cordial hospitality as friend and minstrel, for which friendly reception Malvolio and Barbarino profess a deep appreciation, and to make themselves agreeable they sing a rollicking duet, praising the enlivening effects of wine:

"Fat to the brim the flowing bowl,
With sparkling wine that cheers the soul."

Having thus contributed to the entertainment, the two desperadoes ask Stradella to grant them the favor of a song, since they have made this long journey with the hope of hearing his voice, which it has been told is of matchless melody. With prompt courtesy Stradella replies:

"With all my heart, Salvator Rosa's song I'll render,
If all this company will their good help tender."

Thereupon Stradella advances and renders one of the most delightful numbers of the opera, known as the "Bandit Ballad," in which the chorus joins. The song is a recitative, in that unconsciously Stradella relates therein his own situation, as the object of criminal intent upon the part of robbers who for wealth hesitate at no deed. But he has a good word for even such as these, whose virtue lies in the discrimination which the freebooter exercises in his forays, respecting the fair, compassionating the poor, sympathizing with the lover, and taking only that which the rich can spare. Thus:

"This world to which our fate is bound
Is not so bad as some would make it.
E'en robbers, it is said, have found
That all depends on how we take it."

This sentiment, as well as the song, is vigorously applauded and begets the admiration of Malvolio and Barbarino, who repent their designs upon Stradella's life and join heartily in the refrain:

"Noble art its recognition
Everywhere on earth shall find.
Even bandits feel its mission
And turn their hearts towards mankind!"

which ballad, and a chorus song, "Fill, fill," conclude the second act.

Act III opens with a song by Stradella and Leonora in praise of fair Italia, land of soft verdure, kissed by fragrant winds, laved by sapphirine seas, spanned by azure skies, home of minstrelsy, and heart of splendid antiquity. This lyrical exaltation arouses a patriotic feeling in Malvolio and Barbarino, who enter before the song is finished, and each, in turn, renders a similar tribute. Barbarino has special love for Spezia, his native town, and for Toscana, the fair Phœbe who pours his wine. Malvolio finds no other place on earth so worthy of man's praise as Naples, famed for blue skies, rich wines and beautiful women, while for that which entertains both sight and taste, no where else is the Tarantella danced so joyously, nor is macaroni so plentiful elsewhere. These songs of tribute and levity are followed by the chorus admonishing that the morning beams are pouring upon Madonna's shrine, which is reminder to pay devotions too long neglected. Leonora and Stradella resolve to repair immediately to the shrine, their sacred duty to perform, but Malvolio and Barbarino remain behind a few moments to indulge their gambling propensities, which they do by casting dice; Malvolio, however, is always the winner and Barbarino, with some show of vexation, refuses to continue the play while ill-luck runs so hard against him. As the two go out a choral chant is heard:

"With hope and faith each pilgrim presses
Towards the shrine with fervent heart."

Bassi now cautiously enters the empty room and peering about to discover if any one is present, or if there be signs of an encounter, which he hopes to find, he recites to himself. "What a strange silence! I wonder if the deed is finished; if my full vengeance has fallen upon the singer who has despoiled me of my ward? Ah, if I could but know that his dying chant is ended! Hush! Some one comes. I must conceal myself!"

As Bassi retires behind a screen Malvolio and Barbarino reappear, who fall to discussing the deed which Bassi has hired them to execute. Malvolio is first to speak, who asks his companion what he thinks about the bargain? Barbarino hesitates to express an opinion, preferring that Malvolio shall declare himself. Whereupon Malvolio in a spirit of magnanimity, offers to allow Barbarino the honor of doing the deed and to keep the entire reward. The two indulge in an exciting disputation, each declaring that the other shall perform the crime, until the loud contention is arrested by the coming of Bassi upon the scene, who has heard all from his hiding place. Bassi rails at the men as cowards, and as cheats, but Malvolio and Barbarino return to him the gold he has paid them, confessing that they have not earned it and have no disposition to keep money stained by dishonesty. The three render an exquisite terzetto of complaining, accusing, and explaining, in which Bassi protests that he has been tricked, and the two bravoes declare their conscience has made them cowards but not knaves.

Presently, to end the dispute, Malvolio says he must hurry to his wife to avoid a scolding, and Barbarino excuses himself by announcing that he must hasten home to nurse the baby. Bassi, distracted by their refusal to perform the deed agreed upon, offers to double the reward, but his bribe is refused, and the two taunt him:

"Ah, if the lover
Perchance discover
The guardian's design,
He'd run a knife though him,
He'd put an end to him—
A punishment condign."

Bassi, alarmed over his own situation, jeopardized by the chance of exposure, continues to increase his offers, "ten ducats, twenty ducats, fifty ducats, aye, two hundred ducats, will I give you!" "You must remember," answers Malvolio, "good singers like Stradella are rarely to be found." "Aye, aye," interposes Barbarino, "any stage director able to employ him, would pay double your price, thereby to save him. Wait until he loses his voice and the job may be done cheaper." Bassi, with show of great passion, offers three hundred ducats for the deed. This is so tempting that the desperadoes cease their levity, and consider the proposal, but conclude to refuse it, whereupon his fear, anger and passionate love for Leonora prompts Bassi to tender the bravoes four hundred ducats upon condition that they do the deed quickly and bring back to him the fair one. Malvolio and Barbarino have so little conscience between them that it cannot withstand so great an enticement, and promise to kill Stradella if two hundred ducats be given them in advance, and the remainder be paid upon proof of the crime.

As the compact is completed by payment of the gold, a noise is heard outside which they have no doubt is Stradella returning to his house to rehearse his hymn to the Virgin. The

three conspirators though reluctant to perform a deed which appears like striking a friend, before retiring encourage themselves for the affair in hand by singing:

    "Softly watch we; not one word
    Must from either one be heard!
    Hide we now, and fear dispel.
    Singer, lover, fare thee well."

As the trio conceal themselves Stradella comes upon the scene, and with devotion marking his tones he sings:

    "How sweetly dawns the day,
    Bright his beams are gleaming;
    Joy seems to mark the way,
    And all our prospects pleasing!
    Madonna, at your shrine I pray,
    Give me faith to know the way."

While Stradella is rehearsing his hymn to the Madonna, Bassi entreats the assassins to perform the deed. "What," answers Malvolio, "stab him while he is praying!" "So much better is the opportunity," presses Bassi. Barbarino declares it is vain for him to dissemble his fears, and Malvolio confesses that he is trembling with horror at the thought of what he has engaged to do. Bassi still urges commission of the crime, and appeals to their promise, and love of money, of which latter he has pledged to give them a goodly store, but to all induce-

ments the two assassins show indifference before the guileless object of Bassi's vengeance, whose melodious voice, and generous disposition, has dulled the edge of cupidity. Barbarino answers Bassi's insistence by pleading for delay, that they may hear Stradella's matchless song to its conclusion, which, however, grows more entrancing and gradually dissuades them from their purpose as he sings of hardened sinners whom doubt has enslaved, who scorned and detested must perish for aye, but for such he implores grace, that they may be brought on bended knees to confess their guilt, and by deeds of expiation gain pardon and redemption through a Saviour's love. Bassi importunes so pressingly that several times Malvolio and Barbarino are almost persuaded to strike their drawn daggers into the singer's back, but are restrained by accusing conscience, and presently renounce their criminal intent and join in a finale:

    "Holy Virgin, grant consolation
    To all who are by guilt oppressed;
    May they by deeds of expiation
    Cleanse their hearts of sin confessed."

Surprised by the interruption, Stradella turns to ask who has thus intruded upon his devotions, and receives his answer from Leonora, who, alarmed, tells him it is her guardian. Recognizing Malvolio and Barbarino, who stand before him objects of contrition, though with daggers in their hands, he seeks explanation of their presence in his house, armed as if intent upon some desperate purpose. To this the two bravoes frankly confess that their intent has been to kill him, but that his song has averted the crime they contemplated, and that now they implore his forgiveness, with hope to be called henceforth his friends. They then offer to return the blood money which Bassi has paid them for a deed unperformed, but he refuses to receive the gold, and with a show of generosity bids them keep it, for which gift they express thanks. At

STRADELLA.

this moment a party of pilgrims and citizens come upon the scene to offer congratulations and pay homage to the newly wedded pair, to Stradella, sweetest of singers, to Leonora, fairest of maids, which they perform by rendering in chorus a devotional chant:

" With pious hearts we here assemble,
To await the choral train,
Which approach with joy revealing,
Joining in our glad refrain."

The sight of so much happiness contrasted with his own miserable jealousy, compels Bassi to repent his evil ambitions. Realizing now that atonement may be best made by bestowing his blessings, he advances towards Stradella and Leonora with humble bearing, and with uplifted hands piously invokes a benediction upon the wedded couple. The chorus thereupon chants the hymn:

Holy Virgin, we adore thee,
And our praises we bestow;
Blessings grant us, we implore thee,
Thou through whom all blessings flow."

The invocation, blessings, praises, and congratulations of the company, added to the contrition manifested by Malvolio and Barbarino, and the repentant feeling of Bassi, affects Leonora with deep emotion; she cannot be unmindful of the indignities she has suffered at the hands of her unnatural guardian, nor can she excuse the evil designs of the hired assassins who but for conscience pangs would have robbed her of wedded bliss; but with pious resignation and faithful devotion to her religious vows, she expresses the thankfulness of her heart, and with unmeasured mercy she forgives the offences of her enemies and the wrongs of those who plotted her undoing. With such sense of charity does Leonora accept the apologies of Bassi, and consents to restore him to her confidence. Stradella, no less magnanimous, freely pardons those who have been his enemies, having received assurances that these have now become his friends, appreciative of his nobleness of mind as they are admirers of his talent as a minstrel. The chorus now renders an air of thanksgiving, and an offering of adoration to the Holy Virgin, and as the pious song expires, the curtain slowly descends upon a consummation of love's perfect attainment.

www.ingramcontent.com/pod-product-compliance
Lightning Source LLC
Chambersburg PA
CBHW030313170426
43202CB00009B/982